THE NOONDAY DEVIL

JEAN-CHARLES NAULT, O.S.B.

Abbot of Saint-Wandrille

THE NOONDAY DEVIL

Acedia, the Unnamed Evil of Our Times

Foreword by

MARC CARDINAL OUELLET

Prefect of the Congregation for Bishops

Translated by

MICHAEL J. MILLER

IGNATIUS PRESS   SAN FRANCISCO

Original French title:
Le démon de midi—L'acédie,
mal obscur de notre temps
© 2013 by L'Échelle de Jacob, Dijon, France

Unless otherwise indicated, citations from Church
documents are taken from the Vatican website:
www.vatican.va

Cover art:
The Absinthe Drinker
Edgar Degas (1834–1917)
Musee d'Orsay, Paris, France
© Scala/Art Resource

Cover design by Roxanne Mei Lum

Contents

Acknowledgments

I wish to thank the Father Abbot and the monks of Sainte-Anne de Kergonan, who authorized the transcription and publication of these conferences, which were given not long ago in their abbey.

I wish to thank Marie-Françoise and Véronique for their tremendous work of transcribing them for the (French) first edition.

Foreword

Very early on, the monastic tradition became interested in a strange and complex phenomenon: acedia. Spiritual sloth, sadness, and a disgust with the things of God, a loss of the meaning of life, despair of attaining salvation: acedia drives the monk to leave his cell and to flee intimacy with God, so as to seek here and there some compensation for the austere way of life to which he felt called by God. The psychological and spiritual subtlety of those who first studied this phenomenon—the Desert Fathers and Evagrius of Pontus in particular—cannot fail to challenge our contemporaries who, although they are no longer familiar with the term acedia, no doubt still experience the terrible symptoms of it. For acedia, the monastic sin par excellence, is certainly not to be considered as something from another era. On the contrary, might it not be the gloomy evil of our age?

Weariness, melancholy, feeling overworked, discouragement, instability, activism, boredom, or depression: these various manifestations of the "noonday devil" are enough to convince us of the relevance of an evil that causes a man to lose his relish for life and paralyzes his interior dynamism. Left to his own devices, man ultimately despairs of ever being able to find a meaning for his existence and runs the risk of sinking into a mediocrity that is just the symptom of his rejection of his own greatness as an adopted son of God.

This book by Father Jean-Charles Nault, O.S.B., for which I am pleased to write a preface, is a compact presentation, for a broader reading public, of a long study on acedia that I personally found very interesting and enlightening when I read it some years ago. The author had the insight that acedia, against which his monastic formation had warned him, was not just the concern of monks but threatened people in all states of life, and that it directly affected the relationship between men and God. Indeed, far from being mere distraction in prayer or a lazy nonchalance, acedia appeared to him, over the course of the study, to be a terrible evil that directly concerned the ultimate end of human life, that is, participation in the very life of the Trinity. The simple, direct style of the work makes the reader feel involved and challenged to consider anew what is essential in his existence.

In the first chapter, starting from delectable texts by the first monks of the desert, we are led to discover the multiple facets of an obscure malady that the monastic tradition rightly considered one of the most pernicious that can afflict us. Whereas the various manifestations of acedia make us shudder because of their contemporary relevance, the remedies proposed by the Fathers are striking in their simplicity. In reading these pages, we definitely feel very close to those anchorites of the desert!

A second chapter dwells at length on the teaching of Saint Thomas Aquinas, whose perspicacity is not at all diminished when he speaks about acedia. The great theologian of the thirteenth century, heir of the long patristic and monastic tradition, proves to be prophetic when he assigns to acedia a strategic position in our understanding of Christian action. As a sin against the joy that springs from charity, affecting the frontier between the flesh and the spirit, acedia can be considered the major obstacle to enthusiastic Christian witness. Saint Thomas does not hesitate, however, to propose an astonishing method of overcoming it . . .

In the last two chapters, the author examines the current relevance of acedia, first of all in Christian life in general, then in the different states of life. This hitherto unpublished presentation of his research leads us right to the heart of the spiritual and sometimes confused quest of our times. It reminds us of the importance of the spiritual combat in our life and shows us how acedia can threaten the growth and flourishing of the human person.

Confidence, however, has the last word, for, as Evagrius already wrote in the late fourth century, when someone has resisted acedia, "a state of peace and ineffable joy ensues in the soul after this struggle."

Marc Cardinal Ouellet
Prefect of the Congregation for Bishops

Abbreviations

CCL	*Corpus Christianorum Latinorum*
DC	*Documentation catholique*
FOC	Fathers of the Church (series published by Catholic University of America Press)
NPNF-2	Nicene and Post-Nicene Fathers, second series
PG	*Patrologia Graeca* (ed. J. P. Migne)
PL	*Patrologia Latina* (ed. J. P. Migne)
SC	*Sources chrétiennes*
ST	Saint Thomas Aquinas, *Summa Theologiae*

Introduction

Even though the subject was at first the topic of a thesis, this book is the work, not of a "specialist", but rather of a monk who, like the readers and together with them, is trying to seek God unceasingly. In response to repeated requests that he has received to present his reflections on acedia to a wider public, the author gives us here a livelier, more contemporary version of his study. The spoken style, which reflects the conferences on which this book is based, has been preserved.

At Saint Wandrille's Abbey,[1] the monks have preserved the custom of reciting, before study, and most especially before the prayerful study of Sacred Scripture, the traditional invocation to the Holy Spirit, the *Veni sancte Spiritus*: "God, you have instructed the hearts of the faithful by the light of the Holy Spirit; grant that through that same Holy Spirit, we may always be truly wise [literally, *savor* what is right] and *rejoice* in his consolation."

This prayer asks two things of the Holy Spirit: to make us *relish* or *savor* (in Latin: *sapere*) what is right, what is true; and, on the other hand, that we may *rejoice* (in Latin: *gaudere*) in his divine consolation. *Savor* and *joy*: these are

---

[1] The Abbaye de Fontenelle, founded in 649 by Saint Wandrille, a high-ranking dignitary of the Court of King Dagobert, is located on the bank of the Seine River between Rouen and Le Havre. It houses a community of thirty-five Benedictine monks who lead a life of prayer, silence, and work, while following the *Rule* written by Saint Benedict (480–547).

the two poles around which this reflection intends to re-volve.

Let us begin with two quotations. The first is taken from a book on the virtues and the faith, written in 1994 by a moralist from Milan, Father Giuseppe Angelini:

> Overlooked by preachers and catechists, and not even known by the spiritual masters, acedia is absolutely and completely ignored in all works dealing with moral theology.[2]

The second quotation is taken from the retreat preached in 1996 at the Vatican by Cardinal Christoph Schönborn:

> It seems to me that the deepest crisis in the Church today is that we no longer dare to believe in what God can do for the good with those who love him (cf. Rom 8:28). The spiritual masters traditionally call this torpor of mind and heart *acedia*.[3]

Here are two statements that paradoxically appear to be contradictory: on the one hand, acedia is the most for-gotten topic of modern morality; on the other hand, it is perhaps the root cause of the greatest crisis in the Church today.

What prompted me to delve a little into this topic of acedia is precisely my reading of the book by Giuseppe Angelini: *Le virtù e la fede*. On opening it, I discovered the title of the first chapter: "Acedia". That title piqued my interest. I should point out that when someone enters the novitiate, the novice master gives the newcomer several texts on this

---

[2] Giuseppe Angelini, *Le virtù e la fede* (Milan: Glossa, 1994), 65.
[3] C. Schönborn, *Loving the Church: Retreat to John Paul II and the Papal House-hold* (San Francisco: Ignatius Press, 1998), 56.

subject: the *Institutes* of John Cassian, for example, in chapter 10, or the *Praktikos*, a treatise on the ascetic life by Evagrius of Pontus, chapter 12, or else *The Ladder of Divine Ascent* by John Climacus. The notion itself of acedia was therefore not unfamiliar to me, but what I found difficult to understand was the fact that there could be some relation between acedia and the virtues: How could a book dedicated to the virtues start with a chapter on acedia? This chapter cited a very famous passage by Evagrius, to which we will have reason to return; but most importantly, several pages farther on, I was surprised to find a reference to Saint Thomas Aquinas. In the *studium* at Saint-Wandrille, I had studied Saint Thomas a little, but I had no idea at all that he had devoted a question of his *Summa Theologiae* to acedia. For him, acedia was not unimportant, since he labeled it a sin against charity, more precisely the sin against the joy that springs from charity.

I noticed then that Saint Thomas cited four authors: Saint John Damascene, John Cassian, Saint Gregory the Great, and Saint Isidore of Seville. So it was that I had the idea of doing a little study on the monastic and patristic sources of Saint Thomas' teaching on acedia. At that time I could hardly imagine the depths to which that study would lead me! Today I thank God for having brought to completion that work, which was a gift that I received rather than a personal choice. I might add that familiarity with the Fathers of the Church and with Saint Thomas Aquinas is a special grace, which has enabled me to turn this study into an occasion for contemplation and prayer. For this, too, I give thanks to God.

Most of our contemporaries know nothing about acedia. Few people are aware that this is what tradition identified as the famous "noonday devil" feared by those who are going through the well-known "mid-life crisis". However, although the term "acedia" has been forgotten, the phenomenon that it designates has not disappeared. It is enough to delve into the colorful texts of the first monks of the desert to find that out. The very expression "noonday devil" ought to catch our attention. Usually, indeed, the demon is associated with the night and not with broad daylight! Could it be precisely this unexpected character of a demon who comes to attack in the middle of the day that makes acedia a particularly terrible evil? Although the midday sun comes to bathe everything in its dazzling light, acedia, like an obscure malady, plunges the heart of the person that it afflicts into the gray fog of weariness and the night of despair.

I

Evagrius and the Desert Fathers

Let us begin our survey with the one who first presented a coherent doctrine about acedia: Evagrius of Pontus (345–399). In reading his works, we are in a very particular context, that of the "desert". After the Edict of Milan (313), which officially put an end to the persecutions of Christians in the Empire, an extraordinary spiritual movement started in the Church: some Christians, from every social class and all walks of life, traveled to the desert so as to lead there a life of prayer and asceticism in solitude. According to the biblical notion, the desert is simultaneously the place of intimacy with God[1] and the place of spiritual combat.[2] These Christians, who were called the "Desert Fathers", were thus at the origin of the great monastic movement in the Church.

In order to embark on this subject, I propose that we start with two short *apothegms*,[3] or "sayings", colorful words of wisdom derived precisely from the desert tradition.

---

[1] See, for example, what is said in chapter 2 of the Book of the Prophet Hosea (Hos 2:14ff.).

[2] Think, in particular, of the combat that Jesus had to wage against Satan in the desert (Mt 4:1–11; Mk 1:12–13; Lk 4:1–13).

[3] *Apothegms* (or *apophtegmes*) are statements, anecdotes, or sayings attributed to the Desert Fathers who populated Egypt in the fourth century.

Here is the first:

> A brother spent nine years, tempted to leave the *cenobium*.
> Every day he got his things ready to leave, and when eve-
> ning came, he would say to himself: "Tomorrow, I go
> away." In the morning he again thought to himself: "Let
> us strive again to hold out today because of the Lord." And
> when he had spent the nine years in that way, God relieved
> him of that temptation.[4]

And here is the other passage:

> One Saturday that was a feast day, it happened that the
> brothers were eating at the church of the *kelia*, and, as
> they were serving bowls of porridge, Abbot Helladios of
> Alexandria began to weep. Abbot James asked him, "Abba,
> why are you weeping?" He replied: "This is the end of the
> joys of the soul, that is, of fasting; now we have the con-
> tentment of the body."[5]

You see what a concept of joy the Desert Fathers had.
It makes us smile, but, on reflection, it is extraordinary!

Let us return to Evagrius of Pontus, who belongs to the
third generation of the Desert Fathers. It would be interesting to dwell a little on his life, but such a study would
go beyond the parameters of this volume.[6] Let us simply say that Evagrius was one of those men—a relatively
common occurrence in Church history—whose destiny

---

[4] *Anonyme* 207, in *Les Apophtegmes des Pères: Collection systématique (chapitres
I–IX)*, French translation by J.-C. Guy, Sources chrétiennes 387 (Paris: Cerf,
1993), 378.

[5] *Helladios S1*, in *Les Sentences des Pères du désert: Collection alphabétique*
(Solesmes: Éditions de Solesmes, 1981), 329.

[6] About the life of Evagrius, the reader may consult A. Guillaumont, *Un
philosophe au désert, Évagre le Pontique*, Textes et traditions 8 (Paris: Vrin, 2004).

was contradictory in more than one respect:[7] a man of the world at first, then a humble Desert Father; held in great esteem during his lifetime, then discredited for a long time after his death. After a turbulent life, Evagrius became a Desert Father who was full of understanding and truly exceptional goodness, but also strict and uncompromising in his personal life. During his years in the desert, Evagrius composed a prodigious literary output, which was highly esteemed by his numerous friends and disciples. We can say that his literary work allows us to formulate, in a structured, systematic way, the doctrine of the Desert Fathers.

The Eight Wicked Thoughts

In order to understand Evagrius' teaching on acedia, we have to speak for a moment about the Eastern [Christian] theory of the "thoughts of wickedness" or *logismoi*. We find it in one of the most famous works by Evagrius: the *Praktikos* or *The Monk: A Treatise on the Practical Life*.[8] In the writings of Evagrius, the term *logismos* (wicked thought) is almost always used in the plural, *logismoi*, and in a pejorative sense. The "wicked thought", in his view, is practically identified with the demon who inspires it. Thus most of the time Evagrius speaks about the "demon of

[7] The reader may consult: Palladius, *The Lausiac History*, trans. Robert T. Meyer, Ancient Christian Writers 34 (Westminster, Md.: Newman Press, 1965), chap. 38, pp. 110–13.

[8] Evagrius of Pontus, *Praktikos*, or *The Monk: A Treatise on the Practical Life*, in *Evagrius of Pontus: The Greek Ascetic Corpus*, trans. with introduction and commentary by Robert E. Sinkewicz, Oxford Early Christian Studies (Oxford and New York: Oxford Univ. Press, 2003), 91–114 at 99.

acedia", the "demon of luxury" or the "demon of anger", and so on. The thoughts are practically personified, which makes them quite vivid and enables him to have them "debate" among themselves. This can be found again, several centuries later, in the writings of the Cistercian Galand de Reigny, who, in the thirteenth century, would imagine speeches uttered by the "thoughts".[9]

Evagrius is the first to speak systematically about a doctrine of eight thoughts of wickedness. Why eight? The sources of Evagrius have been the subject of numerous studies and numerous disputes. We cannot enter here into this debate. Let us be content with a few notes. For the sake of brevity, we can say that Origen[10] is certainly the chief schoolmaster of Evagrius and, in that capacity, an indispensable source for him. Moreover, at the death of Evagrius in 499, the so-called "Origenist" crisis started, during which Evagrius was posthumously condemned and most of his writings were hunted down so as to be destroyed. Several survive thanks to the use of pseudonyms, "Nilus of Ancyra" in particular.

The doctrine of the eight thoughts of wickedness originated with a biblical passage, the beginning of chapter 7 of Deuteronomy, which gives the list of the nations that Israel must fight before it can enter the Promised Land. Here is the list: the Hittites, the Girgashites, the Amorites, the Canaanites, the Perizzites, the Hivites, and the

---

[9] Cf. Galand de Reigny, *Parabolaire*, SC 378 (Paris: Cerf, 1992).

[10] Origen (185–253) is one of the greatest Fathers of the Church, often regarded as the Saint Augustine of Greek patristic literature. He can be considered the father of biblical exegesis.

Jebusites (cf. Deut 7:1). Seven nations, to which we must add Egypt, which Israel left by departing for the desert. In all, eight nations, eight enemies that the people of Israel must fight before entering the Promised Land.

Traditional spirituality has always regarded the Christian life as a march through the desert. We left Egypt (that is, the land of sin) by crossing the Red Sea (that is, baptism), and then we began a spiritual itinerary that will last our whole life; it can be likened to a veritable pilgrimage in the desert. In order to be able to enter the Promised Land (that is, eternal life), we must fight several enemies. These eight nations symbolize the eight enemies of the soul that we must combat before experiencing definitive union with God. The worst of these nations is Egypt; the worst of our enemies is pride. As for the other seven enemies to be fought, they are: gluttony, lust or fornication, avarice or greed, sadness, anger, acedia, and vainglory.

Evagrius is the first to present the wicked thoughts always in the same order, with pride at the end of the list. We might say that Evagrius starts with the most carnal wicked thoughts (gluttony and lust) and works his way to the more spiritual ones (vanity and pride). In his view, the thoughts are linked together: gluttony, for example, inclines us to lust, which then requires money in order to be put into action (Evagrius has in mind here resorting to prostitutes), whence greed for gain; but if someone has no money, he falls into sadness, then into anger, acedia, and so on.

All these *logismoi*, according to Evagrius, have essentially a twofold origin, which corresponds to the twofold nature of man, corporeal and spiritual. They come from the two impassioned faculties of the soul, namely, the *concupiscible* [11] and the *irascible*. [12] They arise and darken the third faculty: the *intellect*, the principal function of which is to know God.

All these thoughts come from one or another of the different faculties of the soul, but acedia holds a very special place among them, because it is arises from all the faculties at once, and hence its terrible character. It is found, we could say, at the intersection of two series of vices: one that comes from below (the corporeal passions) and the other that comes from above (the spiritual passions). Acedia affects the body and the soul simultaneously. It takes advantage of a weakness of the body so as to affect the soul.

Evagrius calls acedia "the complex thought". This complexity is manifested likewise in the terminology. It is not insignificant that the word "acedia" has disappeared from the contemporary vocabulary. Certainly, starting with the year 2000 we observe something of a reappearance of the term. But in the specialized literature, in the dictionaries of theology and of spirituality, the word does not appear; it is not defined. Now every time we try to translate this term, we lose a bit of its richness: we speak about languor, torpor, despair, laziness, boredom, or disgust, but ultimately none of these words succeeds in rendering the wealth of connotations of the term *akèdia*. This is why John Cassian, who introduced the doctrine of Evagrius in the West in

[11] The concupiscible appetite is the impassioned faculty of the soul by which we sense an attraction to what appears to us as a good (even if it is a false good).

[12] The irascible appetite, in contrast, is the impassioned faculty of the soul by which we sense aversion to what appears to us as an evil (even if it is in reality a good).

the early fifth century, chose not to translate the Greek term *akèdia* into Latin but to transliterate it as *acedia*. This is why we, too, will keep and use the term "acedia".

Acedia is a formidable danger: whereas the other thoughts are like the links of a chain, acedia is the last of these links: therefore, it is not a transitional evil. Acedia endures. It is not a short-lived crisis. It is a radical, chronic evil. In Evagrius' view, it causes a stifling of the intellect, the *noûs*, whose function is precisely to contemplate God. Starting from the basest passions, it manages to stifle this contemplation of God. However, since this demon is not followed by any other, at least not immediately, victory over it is marvelous.

An Initial Definition?

It is important to return for a moment to the etymology of the word "acedia". Acedia in English comes from the Latin *acedia*, which in turn comes from the Greek *akèdia*. This word means "lack of care". I refer the reader to the works by the Franciscan Bernard Forthomme, who wrote a thick volume on acedia.[13] In a brilliant article, he explained how acedia, before the Christian era, and even before Empedocles (490–435 B.C.) or Cicero (106–43 B.C.), denoted the act of not burying one's dead.[14] This lack of concern for the deceased was an essential characteristic of dehumanization. Indeed, only men bury their dead;

[13] B. Forthomme, *De l'acédie monastique à l'anxio-dépression: Histoire philosophique de la transformation d'un vice en pathologie* (Paris: Sanofi-Synthélabo, 2000).

[14] B. Forthomme, "Émergence et résurgence de l'acédie", in N. Nabert, *Tristesse, acédie et médecine des âmes* (Beauchesne, 2005), 15–35.

animals do not. Not to bury one's dead is therefore an evil especially contrary to the human condition. With Evagrius a new meaning appears: it is no longer about a lack of care with regard to the deceased; it is about a lack of care given to one's own spiritual life, a lack of concern for one's salvation. In Latin, *akèdia* is sometimes translated also by *incuria*, carelessness, indifference.

Evagrius gives no definition of acedia, except on one occasion: he says that it is an *atonia* or "relaxation of the soul", [15] in other words, a lack of spiritual energy. Usually he is content to give a description of it, as is the case in the two following passages, which have not aged in the least, despite the centuries:

> The demon of acedia, also called the noonday demon (cf. Ps. 90:6 Douay-Rheims), is the most oppressive of all the demons. He attacks the monk about the fourth hour [viz. 10 A.M.] and besieges his soul until the eighth hour [2 P.M.]. First of all, he makes it appear that the sun moves slowly or not at all, and that the day seems to be fifty hours long. Then he compels the monk to look constantly towards the windows, to jump out of the cell, to watch the sun to see how far it is from the ninth hour [3 P.M.], to look this way and that lest one of the brothers . . . [might have the good idea of coming to distract him from the monotony of his cell!]. And further, he instils in him a dislike for the place and for his state of life itself, for manual labour, and also the idea that love has disappeared from among the brothers and there is no one to console him. And should there be someone during those days who has offended the monk, this too the demon uses to add further to his dislike (of the place). He leads him on to a desire for other places where he can easily find the wherewithal to meet his needs

---

[15] Evagrius of Pontus, *On the Eight Thoughts* 13, in *Greek Ascetic Corpus*, 83.

and pursue a trade that is easier and more productive; he adds that pleasing the Lord is not a question of being in a particular place: for scripture says that the divinity can be worshipped everywhere (cf. John 4:21–4). He joins to these suggestions the memory of his close relations and of his former life; he depicts for him the long course of his lifetime, while bringing the burdens of asceticism before his eyes; and, as the saying has it, he deploys every device in order to have the monk leave his cell and flee the stadium. No other demon follows immediately after this one: a state of peace and ineffable joy ensues in the soul after this struggle.[16]

Another short passage, taken from the treatise *On the Eight Thoughts* [*of Wickedness*], is even more amusing:

The eye of the person afflicted with acedia stares at the doors continuously, and his intellect imagines people coming to visit. The door creaks and he jumps up; he hears a sound, and he leans out the window and does not leave it until he gets stiff from sitting there. When he reads, the one afflicted with acedia yawns a lot and readily drifts off into sleep; he rubs his eyes and stretches his arms; turning his eyes away from the book, he stares at the wall and again goes back to reading for awhile; leafing through the pages, he looks curiously for the end of texts, he counts the folios and calculates the number of gatherings. Later, he closes the book and puts it under his head and falls asleep, but not a very deep sleep, for hunger then rouses his soul and has him show concern for its needs.[17]

Obviously, this description reflects life in the desert. As you might imagine, between ten o'clock in the morning and two in the afternoon in the Egyptian desert, the sun

---

[16] Evagrius of Pontus, *Praktikos* 12, p. 99.
[17] Evagrius of Pontus, *Eight Thoughts* 14, p. 84.

is at its zenith. Time stands still. Here we see the first dimension of acedia, which is the *temporal* dimension. We will return to it. The day seems to be fifty hours long. The passage of time is never-ending. In those days they ate only once a day, and not very well, either. Even if the monks ate roots—which provided some variety, all things considered—it was nevertheless rather meager fare. Between the heat and the hunger, a certain physical weakness could ensue, accompanied by the potential for a psychological disturbance.

The second dimension is the *spatial* dimension: the impression of being hemmed in, of being stifled. The monk did not go out of his little cell made of branches. When a person had lived in the palaces of kings, it was a bit austere. There was a great temptation, therefore, to go to the window to get a bit of fresh air, a bit of space.

The Five Principal
Manifestations of Acedia

We can reduce the principal manifestations of acedia to five. We will present them in order of increasing intensity and gravity, illustrated at each step of the way by several short passages by Evagrius.

A certain interior instability

The first and surest indication of acedia is a certain interior instability. It is characterized by the need to move about, to have a change of scenery:

Against the thought of listlessness that shows us other places and advises us to acquire a cell there on the pretext that there we will be able to meet our needs without toil and [to provide] peace and consolation to the brothers who come to us.[18]

Or this passage:

The demon of acedia suggests to you ideas of leaving, the need to change your place and your way of life. He depicts this other life as your salvation and persuades you that if you do not leave, you are lost.[19]

Many pretexts, some of them excellent, are given as well under the guise of extraordinary charity, such as visiting the sick, for example:

The spirit of acedia drives the monk out of his cell. . . . A person afflicted with acedia proposes visiting the sick, but is fulfilling his own purpose. A monk given to acedia is quick to undertake a service, but considers his own satisfaction to be a precept. (*Eight Thoughts*, 6, 5, and 6–7)

This can also be the pretext of fulfilling duties to one's family:

Thoughts of listlessness . . . shake our endurance and provoke us to take a little break and make an extended visit to our home and kinfolk. (*Antirrhêtikos* VI, 39)

[18] Evagrius of Pontus, *Antirrhêtikos* VI, 33, in W. Frankenberg, *Evagrius Ponticus* (Berlin, 1912), 472–545. English trans.: Evagrius of Pontus, *Talking Back: A Monastic Handbook for Combating Demons*, trans. David Brakke (Trappist, Ky.: Cistercian Publications; Collegeville, Minn.: Liturgical Press, 2009), citation at 140.

[19] Evagrius of Pontus, *De octo vitiosis cogitationibus* 12, as quoted by P. Miquel, *Lexique du désert: Étude de quelques mots-clés du vocabulaire monastique grec ancien* (Bellefontaine, 1986), 21.

Or else the pretext of serving the living God. Indeed,

[The demon] adds that pleasing the Lord is not a question
of being in a particular place: for scripture says that the divinity can be worshipped everywhere (cf. John 4:21–4).
(*Praktikos* 12)

In other words: the important thing is to adore the Lord
"in spirit and in truth".

We see here that Evagrius presents the person afflicted
with acedia as a "runaway", as a deserter who flees the
spiritual battlefield. As the remedy for it he prescribes *perseverance*, which very often consists of remaining physically
in one's cell, whatever the cost, since physical stability is
designed to support the stability of the heart. The fundamentally important thing is to set one's heart on God.[20]

We know, however, that the Desert Fathers paid each
other visits to seek counsel. Confinement to one's cell was
therefore not absolute.

An exaggerated concern for one's health

Acedia can manifest itself also in an exaggerated concern
for one's physical health, augmented by the precariousness
of the desert, which caused the monk to fear that he would
lack even the essentials:

The thought of listlessness . . . depicts to us a prolonged
old age, severe poverty without consolation, and diseases
that can kill the body. (*Antirrhêtikos* VI, 32)

[20] This reminds me of an anecdote: at Saint Anselm's in Rome there was a
monk who was out and about all the time. One day I met him on the bus.
I had crossed paths with him three times already that same day, outside the
monastery. I then said to him jokingly, "What about stability?" He replied,
"I have my stability in the Heart of Jesus!"

It manifests itself also in temptations to gluttony. Surely the noonday devil found easy prey in the anchorite who fasted until around three in the afternoon and who could legitimately consider his diet a bit austere: "for hunger then rouses his soul and has him show concern for its needs" (*Eight Thoughts* 6, 15).

Later authors, moreover, often showed the connection between the demon of gluttony and acedia. Let us cite, for example, this very humorous passage by Saint John Climacus, a Syrian monk of the sixth or seventh century:

> At the third hour the devil of tedium [acedia] causes shivering, headache, and vertigo. By the ninth hour, the patient has recovered his strength, and when dinner is ready, he jumps out of bed.[21]

Aversion to manual work

A third manifestation of acedia may be a certain aversion to manual work. It must be said that this work, in the desert, was not very enjoyable. They made baskets and then used to go sell them in Alexandria. And if they did not need to sell them, they used to do as Penelope did: they would unmake at night what they had made during the day! It is understandable also that the simple, repetitive work, which was done precisely in order to leave the mind free to devote itself to the Lord, could from time to time appear a bit austere or monotonous:

[21] John Climacus, *The Ladder of Divine Ascent* 13, 8 (PG 88:859), trans. Colm Luibheid and Norman Russell (New York: Paulist Press, 1982), 163.

Acedia is an ethereal friendship, one who leads our steps
astray, hatred of industriousness.[22]

John Cassian, in the next generation, would develop in
particular this question about manual work. It is largely ow-
ing to him that acedia turned into "laziness". Saint Benedict, although he is situated along this line of tradition,
would have the genius to restore to acedia its full significance.

Evagrius, for his part, displays great psychological subtlety. He knows that in contrast to laziness there can also
be a form of activism that consists of fleeing ahead, a flight
from God and from oneself. For true charity begets meekness, while activism begets bitterness.[23]

Neglect in observing the rule

A fourth manifestation of acedia is negligence in carrying
out one's monastic duties, in the first place, prayer. Here
the temptation of "minimalism" creeps in, whereby everything seems to be "too much":

> The monk afflicted with acedia is lazy in prayer and will
> not even say the words of a prayer. As a sick man cannot
> carry about a heavy burden, so the person afflicted by ace-
> dia will not perform a work of God [with diligence]. (*Eight
> Thoughts* 6, 16)

[22] Evagrius of Pontus, *On the Vices Opposed to the Virtues*, in *Greek Ascetic
Corpus*, 60–65 at 64.

[23] The reader may refer to the very fine book by Gabriel Bunge, *Dragon's
Wine and Angel's Bread: The Teaching of Evagrius Ponticus on Anger and Meekness*,
trans. Anthony P. Gythiel (Crestwood, N.Y.: St. Vladimir's Seminary Press,
2009).

And elsewhere:

> The thought of listlessness . . . deprives us of reading and
> instruction in spiritual words, leading us astray as it says,
> "Look, such-and-such holy old man knew only twelve
> Psalms, and he pleased God." (*Antirrhêtikos* VI, 5)

But Evagrius, always the subtle observer, knows very
well that this temptation can ultimately lead to another
temptation, that of "maximalism", since opposites always
meet.[24]

> The demon of acedia . . . suggest[s] to the persevering (as-
> cetic) an extreme withdrawal, inviting him to rival John
> the Baptist and Antony, the very first of the anchorites,
> so that, unable to bear the prolonged and inhumane with-
> drawal, he flees with shame, abandoning the place, and
> the demon then makes his boast, "I prevailed over him"
> (Ps. 12:5).[25]

Other later passages would recall the same teaching:

> To do more than one can, whether works of charity or
> other sorts, is to lack discernment, and that then leads to
> trouble and to murmuring.[26]

---

[24] Evagrius writes with extraordinary psychological subtlety. The reader
may consult A. Grün, *Aux prises avec le mal: Le combat contre les démons dans le
monachisme des origines*, SO 49 (Bellefontaine, 1990). This book draws a comparison between Evagrius and Jung. The author shows how all the insights
of the psychoanalysts are already present in Evagrius.

[25] Evagrius of Pontus, *On Thoughts* 35, 24–30, in *Greek Ascetic Corpus*, 136–
82 at 178.

[26] Barsanuphe et Jean de Gaza, *Correspondance*, letter 621 (Solesmes, 1972),
415.

Again, this short passage by John Climacus has the demon of acedia speak:

> "I have many mothers—Stolidity of Soul, Forgetfulness of
> the Things of Heaven or, sometimes, Too Heavy a Burden
> of Troubles."[27]

General discouragement

If the monk has not abandoned his cell, acedia then will
manage to provoke a state of general discouragement that
can go so far as to call his vocation into question. Finally,
if the monk has seen that it is impossible for him to flee his
painful situation, it may happen that he sinks into a genuine nervous depression, the symptoms of which Evagrius
describes with disturbing precision:

> The soul . . . , due to the thoughts of sloth and listless-
> ness that have persisted in it, has become weak, has been
> brought low, and has dissipated in the miseries of its soul;
> whose strength has been consumed by its great fatigue;
> whose hope has nearly been destroyed by this demon's
> force; that has become mad and childish with passionate
> and doleful tears; and that has no relief from anywhere.
> (*Antirrhêtikos* VI, 38)

Acedia then urges the monk to abandon the holy way of
the heroes, the place where he is residing. This is the short
passage that I cited for you a moment ago, from chapter
12 of the *Praktikos*: "he deploys every device in order to
have the monk leave his cell and flee the stadium", in other
words, abandon the place of spiritual battle. Evagrius mentions two possibilities at that moment: either one flees, or

[27] John Climacus, *The Ladder of Divine Ascent* 13, 8 (PG 88:861A); English
trans. (New York: Paulist Press, 1982), 163–64.

one tries not to flee, but one is then prone to regress in one's behavior and to return to a childish state.

This summary presentation of the different manifestations of acedia, as we find them in the works of Evagrius, shows us how complex and contradictory a phenomenon acedia is. Moreover, Evagrius explains that the danger of acedia is precisely the fact that it conceals itself from the one who experiences it.

The Five Remedies for Acedia

Now we must turn to the remedies, which incidentally are astonishingly simple. Here again, they can be reduced to five. I list them before elaborating on them, and then I will try to find for each one a short passage, taken from Evagrius or from the *Sayings of the Desert Fathers*: tears; prayer and work; the *antirrhêtikos* method, or contradiction; meditation on death, or "the exercise of death"; and finally, perseverance.

Tears

I will start with tears. For Evagrius—and for the whole Eastern spiritual tradition—they have an *initial essential meaning*: they are the acknowledgment that one needs to be saved, that one cannot go it alone. The little child weeps when he is discouraged, when he needs help, when he needs to be loved. The same goes for adults who, somewhere deep down, remain children. To weep is to acknowledge that one needs to be saved. Now, you remember that the word *akèdia* means precisely the lack of concern for one's salvation. Tears are therefore a remedy for acedia, inasmuch as they are the physical, external manifestation of the fact that one needs to be saved. We find this again in the first saying of the *Alphabetical Collection*, attributed to Saint Antony. Antony says: "I want to be saved, but my thoughts do not let me go." In reality, in saying that he wants to be saved, he has already, somewhere, conquered the demon of acedia!

But tears have a *second meaning*: they are like water that falls on a hard rock and, over time, manages to penetrate it. They are like water that flows over the shell of our stony heart, so that it might become a heart of flesh. Little by little they will transform our heart so as to make it docile to the Lord. They will make a notch so that mercy might pour into that gap, into that wound, just as the mercy of God was engulfed in Christ's wound of love on the Cross.[28]

Here is a short passage by Evagrius:

> When we come up against the demon of acedia, then with tears let us divide the soul and have one part offer consolation and the other receive consolation. And sowing within ourselves goodly hopes, let us chant with holy David this incantation: "Why are you saddened, O my soul, and why do you trouble me? Hope in God; for I shall confess him, the salvation of my face and my God" [Ps 41:6]. (*Praktikos* 27)

---

[28] Concerning this doctrine of compunction in Eastern Christianity, I refer the reader to the marvelous book by Irénée Hausherr, *Penthos: The Doctrine of Compunction in the Christian East*, trans. Anselm Hufstader (Kalamazoo, Mich.: Cistercian Publications, 1982).

Here is another one, from *Exhortation to a Virgin*:

Sadness is burdensome and acedia is irresistible, but tears shed before God are stronger than both.[29]

Prayer and work

I will return first to the saying of Antony of which I have already spoken. I refer you to a very fine article by Rémi Brague in the 1985 issue of the *Revue Thomiste*, which unfortunately is too little known: "The Image and Acedia".[30] It is an analysis of this first saying.

Once when Antony was [sitting] in the desert [he fell into] boredom and irritation [*akèdia*]. He said to God, "Lord, I want to be made whole and my thoughts do not let me. What am I to do about this trouble, how shall I be cured?" After a while he got up and went outside. He saw someone like himself sitting down and working, then standing up to pray; then sitting down again to make a plait of palm leaves, and standing up again to pray. It was an angel of the Lord sent to correct Antony and make him vigilant. He heard the voice of the angel saying, "Do this and you will be cured." When he heard it he was very glad and recovered his confidence. He did what the angel had done, and found the salvation that he was seeking.[31]

First of all, it is important to note that, as in the passage from the *Praktikos* by Evagrius, this one ends with joy.

[29] Evagrius of Pontus, *Exhortation to a Virgin* 39, in *Greek Ascetic Corpus*, 131–35 at 134.

[30] R. Brague, "L'image et l'acédie", *Revue Thomiste* 85 (1985): 197–228.

[31] *Antoine* 1 (SC 387:336). English trans. in *The Desert Fathers: Sayings of the Early Christian Monks*, trans. and with an introduction by Benedicta Ward (London: Penguin Books, 2003), 60.

There are many things to be said about this passage. Here I would simply like to emphasize the alternation between prayer and work, which we find again in the writings of Saint Benedict. This is an extraordinary equilibrium of which Evagrius is the champion.

We cite now a short passage from Evagrius:

> Give thought to working with your hands, if possible both night and day, so that you will not be a burden to anyone, and further that you may be able to offer donations, as the holy apostle Paul advised (1 Thess. 2:9; 2 Thess. 3:8). In this way you can also overcome the demon of acedia and eliminate all the other desires inspired by the enemy. The demon of acedia lies in wait for laziness and "is full of desires," as scripture says (Prov. 13:4).[32]

Elsewhere Evagrius also says:

> Perseverance is the cure for acedia, along with the execution of all tasks with great attention [and the fear of God]. Set a measure for yourself in every work and do not let up until you have completed it. (*Eight Thoughts*, 6, 17–18)

The antirrhêtic method, or contradiction

This remedy is quite simple, despite the rather difficult expression by which it is designated. The Greek word *antirrhêsis* means "contradiction". This is about confronting the temptation of acedia by using the method that Christ utilized in the desert against Satan, in other words, the use of a verse from Scripture to confound the devil. Evagrius

---

[32] Evagrius of Pontus, *The Foundations of Monastic Life* 8, in *Greek Ascetic Corpus*, 1–11 at 9.

wrote a work dedicated to this subject that is entitled, precisely, *Antirrhêtikos*. This work was recently translated into English as *Talking Back*. With regard to the eight principal vices discussed earlier, Evagrius specifies all the verses from Scripture that can be used to resist the tempter. Chapter 6 of this work is entirely dedicated to acedia.

The idea of the selection is simple: if the wicked thought tells you such and such, you must reply with this Scripture verse. Saint Benedict, in his *Rule*, would later adopt this principle, formulating it as follows: "When evil thoughts come into one's heart, to dash them against Christ immediately."[33] We find here again the traditional spiritual interpretation of Psalm 137:8–9: "O daughter of Babylon, you devastator! . . . Happy shall he be who takes your little ones and dashes them against the rock!" Babylon is the city of the devil; the rock is Christ. To dash the children of Babylon against the rock is to dash wicked thoughts against Christ as soon as they appear and are still very little. Here, the power of the Word is what comes to our aid in the combat.

John Cassian had already developed this principle in his tenth *Conference*. Whatever thought may come to mind, Cassian prescribes the repetition of a verse from Psalm 69 [Douay-Rheims]: "O God, come to my assistance; O Lord, make haste to help me." From this general principle, which was widespread among the Desert Fathers, the later Eastern tradition developed the so-called "Jesus prayer", which collects all possible petitions in one formula of biblical origin:

[33] Benedict of Nursia, *Rule of Saint Benedict* 4, 50 [hereafter abbreviated *RB*]. Cited from the English version at www.osb.org/rb/

in a confession to Christ it is the acknowledgment of one's sinfulness, the recognition of the need for salvation, and an appeal for mercy.

Meditation on death

Another remedy suggested by Evagrius is meditating on death. Here again, Saint Benedict in his *Rule* recommends, as one of the instruments of good works, "to keep death daily before one's eyes" (*RB* 4, 47). There is nothing morbid about this. It stands to reason as a simple element of vigilance. As Benedict recalls, the first degree of humility is to live in the presence of God. But most importantly, death is the end of our life, the reason why we other monks entered the monastery, but also the end or goal toward which every Christian is journeying. The Desert Fathers had left the world so as to seek God and encounter him. Evagrius reminds them that the sufferings of the present time cannot be measured against the glory that awaits us (cf. Rom 8:18). This idea above all helps us to fight against *philautia*, or self-love, which Evagrius regards as the root of all sins. The thought of death also makes it possible to counteract self-centeredness absolutely. I told you earlier that there was a temporal dimension to acedia. Now the thought of death, precisely, gives meaning to passing time, restores a linear orientation, gives it a *sense*, in both senses of the word: direction and signification.

Perseverance

Finally, the essential remedy is perseverance, in Greek *hypo-monē*, which is a very active thing. It is an appeal, an increase of fidelity. When you are in a tunnel and you see nothing at all, it is advisable to remain near the handrail; otherwise, without noticing it, you will wander off and get turned around. The handrail is fidelity to one's everyday routine, fidelity to one's rule of life. Perseverance sometimes consists of remaining without doing anything, or else, on the contrary, doing everything that one did not think one had come to do. But ultimately, little matters. What does matter is to endure. As another saying puts it: "If you are hungry, eat; if you want to sleep, sleep; but do not leave your cell!"

By means of these five very simple remedies, Evagrius arms us against all temptations to seek purely human solutions. Everything happens in God's light: the tears are tears in the presence of the Lord; the work is closely bound up with prayer; the battle against wicked thoughts is waged with the Word of God; death is not simply the end of our human life, it is the encounter with the Lord; perseverance, finally, is not stoicism but, rather, long patience in God's sight. It is important to point out this spiritual dimension of acedia, so as to adjust our view of the development of the notion of acedia over time. Indeed, as soon as it is taken out of the context of a spiritual life in God's sight, it begins to lose its full significance and be reduced to one or another of its manifestations.

Acedia in the Sayings

Allow me to add a few words concerning the *Apothegms* or *Sayings*, which present nothing but remedies for acedia. Here there is no well-designed treatise or systematic teaching. The texts that we have are statements that are all shaped by a concrete situation: one brother asks another to help him. We are therefore in exactly the same context as Evagrius, and yet at the same time the formulation is different. Let us be content with rereading a few of these little pearls.

Perseverance in one's cell

A brother said to Arsenius, "What shall I do, abba? My thoughts trouble me, telling me, 'You cannot fast, nor work, nor visit the sick, because even these things are self-ish.'" He saw that the devil had put these thoughts in his mind and said, "Go, eat, drink and sleep, only do not leave your cell: remember that staying in the cell is what keeps a monk on the right path."[34]

A brother said to a hermit, "My thoughts wander, and I am troubled." He answered, "Go on sitting in your cell, and your thoughts will come back from their wanderings. If a she-ass is tethered, her foal skips and gambols all round her but always comes back to the mother. It is like that for any-one who for God's sake sits patiently in his cell. Though his thoughts wander for a time, they will come back to Him again."[35]

Hope for eternal life

A hermit was asked by a brother why, when he stayed in his cell, he suffered boredom [acedia]. He answered, "You have not yet seen the resurrection for which we hope, nor

[34] Arsène 11, in Les Sentences des Pères du désert: Collection alphabétique (Solesmes: Éditions de Solesmes, 1981), 4:25. English trans. in Desert Fathers: Sayings, 69.

[35] Anonyme 198, in Les Apophtegmes des Pères: Collection systématique, SC 387 (Paris: Cerf, 1993), 370. English trans. in Desert Fathers: Sayings, 70.

the torment of fire. If you had seen these, then you would bear your cell without boredom even if it was filled with worms and you were standing in them up to your neck."[36]

Being immersed in our everyday world is what very often prevents us from lifting our minds toward the realities of the world to come.

Another saying:

Someone asked an old man: "What do you do to avoid falling into acedia?" He replied: "Every day I wait for death."[37]

And still another:

Some brothers went to the desert to see a great old man and said to him: "Abba, how can you stay here, where you endure such hardship?" The old man told them: "All the time of hardship that I accept here cannot be compared to a single day of the torments that await sinners in the world to come."[38]

Work and asceticism

Besides the first apothegm of the Alphabetical Collection, which is attributed to Antony and cited above, we quote a little passage from the *Instructions* of Dorotheus of Gaza, a monk in Palestine in the mid-sixth century:

A man could be content merely with a simple pillow, and yet he desires a mattress. Someone has a woolen blanket

[36] *Anonyme* 196, SC 387:370. English trans. in *Desert Fathers: Sayings*, 70.
[37] Anonymous, in *Les Sentences des Pères du désert: Collection alphabétique*, 1:301.
[38] *Anonyme* 193, SC 387:368.

and wants to exchange it for another that is new or nicer, out of frivolity or because of acedia. A man could be content with a coat made of several pieces of cloth, but he craves one made of wool, and perhaps he will even become angry if he does not get it.[39]

Prayer and tears

Let us begin with a saying by a fourth-century Desert Mother, Amma Theodora. Indeed, there were not only Desert Fathers, but also women, who vied with the men in their asceticism and sanctity:

> Amma Theodora also said: "Recollection is truly a great thing for the virgin and for the monk, especially for the young ones. But know that when someone decides to embrace it, the Evil One arrives immediately and oppresses the soul with disgust, discouragement (*acedia*), and obsessive thoughts. . . . But if we are vigilant, all that dissipates. There was a monk who, at the start of the Divine Office, was seized with trembling and fever and a very severe headache. He then said to himself: 'Now I am sick, and I will no doubt die! Let us arise then before dying and recite the office!' As soon as he had finished the office, the fever subsided also. And again afterward, by this reasoning, he used to recite the office and triumphed over the thought."[40]

Evagrius had already stated that one of the pernicious effects of acedia is that the person who experiences it is unaware of it. One of the tricks of this demon is to make sure that the person afflicted by it does not know that he

[39] Dorothée de Gaza, *Instructions* III, 45, SC 92 (Paris: Cerf, 1963), 216.
[40] *Théodora* 3, in *Les Sentences des Pères du désert: Collection alphabétique*, 4:120.

is at the bottom of it. Sometimes it is enough to become conscious that one is prey to acedia in order for it to flee immediately.

> A brother questioned Abba Poemen about acedia, and the old man told him: "Acedia is always there at the beginning, and there is no worse passion. But as soon as a man has recognized it, it is calmed."[41]

Others, in contrast, sometimes find that acedia is tenacious.

> Abba Isaiah asked Abba Macarius: "Tell me a saying." The old man replied: "Flee from men." Abba Isaiah asked him, "What does it mean to flee from men?" The old man told him: "Remain seated in your cell and weep over your sins."[42]

Discretion and moderation

> A brother asked Abba Hierax: "Tell me a saying, how will I be saved?" The old man told him: "Remain seated in your cell; if you are hungry, eat; if you are thirsty, drink; never speak evil of anyone, and you will be saved."[43]

In reading these sayings, we notice that the reputation of great excesses that is attributed to the Desert Fathers ("It is easier to admire than to imitate") is unfounded. Great wisdom is to be found in them.

Another saying:

> Evagrius said, "A wandering mind is strengthened by reading, and prayer. Passion is dampened down by hunger and

---

[41] *Poemen* 149, in ibid., 4:254.

[42] *Macaire* 27, in ibid., 4:182.

[43] *Hiérax* 1, in ibid., 4:147.

work and solicitude. Anger is repressed by psalmody and long-suffering and mercy. But all these should be at the proper times and in due measure. If they are used at the wrong times and to excess, they are useful for a short time. But what is only useful for a short time, is harmful in the long run."[44]

Finally, the fundamental law is obedience.

Syncletica said, "It seems to me that for those who live in monasteries obedience is a higher virtue than chastity, however perfect. Chastity is in danger of pride, obedience has the promise of humility."[45]

This rapid review of the teaching of the Desert Fathers on acedia has brought us, after the doctrine of Evagrius, into the concrete situation of everyday life. No doubt Evagrius remains the ancient author who studied acedia the most within the overall context of the spiritual life, and he succeeded in combining the theoretical and systematic character of his presentation with first-rate psychological subtlety. As for the Desert Fathers, they offer us stories that are full of humor and realism at the same time. These very lifelike scenes have retained all their freshness after fifteen or sixteen centuries.

In the *Apothegms*, acedia appears as the great enemy of solitary life, which manifests itself above all in the temptation to flee one's cell. For the Desert Fathers, this is truly the fundamental characteristic. But it is necessary to understand that persevering in one's cell, which they recommend in season and out of season, means persevering in

[44] *Évagre*, in ibid., 1:135. English trans. in *Desert Fathers: Sayings*, 93.
[45] *Synclétique*, 16, ibid., 1:201; English trans. in *Desert Fathers: Sayings*, 143.

one's resolution to lead the monastic life and to seek perfection. It is the indispensable condition for being united with God and obtaining eternal life. It is the prerequisite for salvation. "Father, what must I do to be saved?" This is the jolting question that runs through all the literature of the desert, inspired by the Gospel verse: "Teacher, what good deed must I do, to have eternal life?" (Mt 19:16).

The Next Few Centuries

Within the parameters of this book we cannot present in detail all the authors who spoke about acedia between the fourth and the twelfth century.[46] Let us be content to present several of the more significant authors.

John Cassian

John Cassian (ca. 360–433) performed the great service of making this doctrine of the Desert Fathers known in the West. It is not known whether Cassian personally met Evagrius. It is possible, but it is not certain. Indeed, Cassian visited the anchorites or hermits in the Egyptian desert for several years and ended his visit in 399, that is, in the year of Evagrius' death. Upon arriving in Marseilles, Cassian set down in writing all his conversations with the hermits of Egypt, which produced the twenty-four *Conferences*. As

[46] For a more detailed study, the reader may refer to: Jean-Charles Nault, *La saveur de Dieu: L'acédie dans le dynamisme de l'agir*, 2nd ed., Cogitatio Fidei 248 (Paris: Cerf, 2010), 75–165.

for acedia strictly speaking, Cassian discusses it mainly in the *Institutes*, a later work in which he presents a semi-eremitical life. Consequently, the manner in which acedia is presented in Cassian's writings differs somewhat from the presentation by Evagrius.

Indeed, in a semi-eremitical setting, the monks are obliged to leave their cell, since there is a modicum of community life. Acedia is therefore not limited to the temptation to leave one's cell. Cassian presents it above all as a lack of impetus to work. In chapter 10 of the *Institutes*, Cassian offers a magnificent literary description of acedia, quite close to the one by Evagrius in its final paragraphs. But very quickly the rest of the chapter turns into an apologia for manual work. Viewed through this prism, acedia becomes tinged with laziness: the remedy prescribed by Cassian is precisely manual work. This modification would have major repercussions over the course of the centuries. Somewhere along the line it is possible to say that Cassian is at the origin of the transformation of acedia into sloth. Moreover, he would influence Saint Benedict to some extent.

Two important points in Cassian's writings must be noted. First of all, his abundant use of medical vocabulary —which the reader will find again, incidentally, in Saint Benedict—leads us to ask whether acedia is a sin or an illness. One could ask the same question while reading chapters 27 and 28 of the *Rule of Saint Benedict*. Nevertheless, Christ himself says in the Gospel: "Those who are well have no need of a physician, but those who are sick. . . . I came not to call the righteous, but sinners" (Mt 9:12–13). This therefore establishes a certain equivalence between those who are well and the righteous and between sick people and sinners. In this sense, illness can truly be understood in the sense of sin.

We have spoken about the passions in the writings of Evagrius, but we have not spoken about personal responsibility. One may wonder, therefore: Is man, in Evagrius' opinion, personally responsible for the acedia that afflicts him? In other words: Can acedia be a sin? In reality, Evagrius does indeed allow room for human freedom. Twice, at least, Evagrius explains his opinion on this point. For example, in chapter 6 of his *Treatise on the Practical Life* we read:

> Whether or not all these thoughts trouble the soul is not within our power; but it is for us to decide [whether] they are to linger within us or not and whether or not they stir up the passions. (*Praktikos* 6)

In the same work, a little farther on, we read: "Sin for a monk is the consent of the thought to the forbidden pleasure" (*Praktikos* 75). He therefore leaves room for personal responsibility. Cassian and Saint Benedict will do the same.

The other important element that we find in Cassian's writings, insofar as they concern acedia, is that he is the first to assign *offspring* to it. Indeed, he attributes "daughters" to various vices. In the case of acedia, he lists eight, namely: laziness, sleepiness, peevishness, restlessness, vagrancy, instability of mind and body, garrulousness, and curiosity.

In conclusion, we should note a minor modification in vocabulary: Evagrius spoke about eight "wicked thoughts" (*logismoi*). Cassian, for his part, speaks about eight "principal vices" (*vitia principalia*). Gregory the Great, two centuries later, would keep the expression "principal vices", although he was acquainted with only seven of them. Finally, in the twelfth century, Hugh of Saint Victor would be the first to talk about the seven "capital sins" (*peccata capitalia*).

Benedict of Nursia

Saint Benedict, patriarch of the monks of the West (480–547), speaks about acedia in chapter 48 of his *Rule*. The extraordinary thing about Saint Benedict's writings is that he situates acedia within the context of *lectio divina*.[47] At the very beginning I quoted the prayer *Veni sancte Spiritus*, which is the traditional prayer before *lectio divina*. One could say that it is a true antidote against acedia, since it asks that we might rediscover a taste for the Word of God and might rejoice in the presence of the Holy Spirit. Saint Benedict grasped particularly well the fact that the strongest desire not to persevere could occur during *lectio divina*. Conversely, during *lectio divina* one can truly discover or rediscover the savor of things, in the long term. We find here a certain conversion of time: the fact of taking time with the Word of God and of rediscovering the joy of this Word.

---

[47] *Lectio divina* can be defined as a prayerful, meditative reading of Scripture, under the prompting of the Holy Spirit. It is not just about *listening* to the Word of God through prayer and meditation; it is also about *responding* by prayer and *putting it into practice* in everyday life. According to the ancient monastic rules, in particular Saint Benedict's, *lectio divina* is, along with liturgical prayer and work, one of the three pillars of monastic life. The monk dedicates a considerable amount of time to it each day.

Gregory the Great

Pope Saint Gregory the Great (540–604) never uses the term "acedia". Nevertheless, Saint Thomas Aquinas later cited him as one of his sources! How can we explain this? What is truly surprising is that Gregory habitually cites Cassian. Why, then, does he not follow him where acedia is concerned? Indeed, in his *Morals on the Book of Job*, Gregory discusses the principal vices extensively. However, he limits himself to a group of seven vices, from which acedia has disappeared. Let us not forget that Saint Gregory is the author who was studied the most during the Middle Ages. During that period the custom developed of drawing up concordance tables of all the elements that are seven in number: the seven gifts of the Holy Spirit, the seven petitions of the Our Father, the seven principal virtues (three theological and four cardinal virtues), the seven beatitudes (according to the reckoning of Saint Augustine, who considered the eighth beatitude to be a summary of the seven others), and finally the seven principal vices.

In these tables, each of the seven vices is associated with a virtue, a petition of the Our Father, a beatitude, and a gift of the Holy Spirit. Gregory the Great, who is very fond of this symbolism, is therefore preoccupied with establishing a group of seven vices. In order to arrive at the number seven, he starts by removing pride, the mother of all the vices. Pride, therefore, is not found on the list, since it is a thing apart. But Gregory is not content with removing pride. He also introduces a new vice, envy (*invidia*). In order to get the number seven, he must therefore again remove a vice. Now the one that Gregory removes is acedia, and only sadness is kept. Already in the writings of Evagrius, sadness and acedia were almost twin sisters. The difference between them was that sadness is transient, while acedia is lasting, deeply engrained. Gregory the Great incorporates acedia into sadness: moreover, the daughters of sadness that he mentions are the ones that Cassian attributed to acedia.

As a result, the term "acedia" disappears entirely. We may wonder why Gregory the Great abolished acedia, when he himself was a monk and knew perfectly well the monastic doctrine on acedia, as transmitted by Cassian. No doubt, in his *Morals on the Book of Job* he was aiming at a non-monastic readership. The meaning of "acedia", in his view, was too specifically monastic and had little significance for his readers. Not until the twelfth century would acedia reappear in the official lists of vices, even though monastic works during that time still continued to denounce the major risk that it poses to a monk's perseverance.

Hugh of Saint Victor

It was left to Hugh of Saint Victor (d. 1141) to make the final transformation in the list of vices. He shared Gregory's preoccupation with having a list of seven elements yet replaced sadness with acedia, while keeping envy. Hugh of Saint Victor's list was the one that Saint Thomas Aquinas had in front of him and used, while mistakenly attributing it to Saint Gregory.

Throughout the Middle Ages, the monks sought to be faithful to Cassian and at the same time to Gregory the

Great. For a long time, there were compromises and attempts to coordinate the two lists of vices. Hugh of Saint Victor deserves credit for resolving the problem by fixing the seven elements. He was also the one who introduced the expression "capital sins" (*peccata capitalia*), which was borrowed from military language: the capital sins or vices are vices that bring along other sins after them, in much the same way as in an army the file leaders have a whole line of soldiers behind them. The expression "capital sins" therefore refers, not to their seriousness, but, rather, to the aptitude of these sins to engender others, which gives them a particularly formidable character.

Saint Thomas Aquinas would align himself decidedly with the Gregorian tradition by considering acedia to be a form of sadness, but a very particular sort: a sadness about God. However, as we will soon see, Saint Thomas would prove to be an indisputably genial and original thinker.

Saint Thomas Aquinas

Preliminary Remarks

Thus far we have seen how the tradition of the desert, thanks above all to Evagrius, brought to light the complex and at the same time terrible phenomenon of acedia as a major obstacle to the flourishing of our spiritual life, of our ability to enter into a relationship with the Lord, to "know" the Lord, in the biblical sense of the word. We saw how it was possible to be delivered from it by humble perseverance in God's sight.

Now we will see how Saint Thomas Aquinas (1224–1274) envisages acedia. Even though the terms of the presentation are altogether different, we will remain very close to Evagrius: the major insights coincide. It is true that Saint Thomas never cites Evagrius. If he knows of him, it is through Cassian. But we must remember that during the Middle Ages Evagrius was considered a heretic. Moreover, Saint Thomas did not know Greek well. That is why he never cites Evagrius. Nevertheless, there are many comparisons to be made between Evagrius and Thomas. Similarly, the analogies between Saint Thomas and Saint Benedict are very important.

We will dwell on the two definitions of acedia that Saint Thomas gives. Here they are: "sadness about spiritual good" (*tristitia de bono divino*) and "disgust with activity" (*taedium operandi*). In order to understand these two definitions correctly, it is necessary to put them back into the context of the moral doctrine of Saint Thomas. We must therefore immerse ourselves for a moment in his thought.

I would like to begin with three preliminary remarks, which we must keep in mind when we take up the work of Saint Thomas:

1. Saint Thomas Aquinas—one of the greatest teachers of theology of all time—is rooted in a tradition that absolutely must be taken into consideration if we do not want to misinterpret his thought. This is why it was important to make the historical survey in the preceding chapter.

2. We will limit ourselves to two fundamental texts by Saint Thomas: question 35 of the *Secunda secundae* (IIa-IIae) of the *Summa Theologiae*,[1] which is made up of four articles; and question 11 of the treatise *De malo*,[2] which also consists of four articles. However, it would be absurd to isolate these two questions from the doctrine of Saint Thomas as a whole.

3. It is necessary to take into account the extraordinary unity that exists, in the thought of Saint Thomas, between our *moral life*—our activity—and our *spiritual life*—our life

[1] The *Summa Theologiae* (Summary of theology)—a better title than *Summa Theologica* (Theological summary)—is the most famous work of Saint Thomas Aquinas. It is one of the grandest theological syntheses of all time, and it was composed during the last seven years of Saint Thomas' life, between 1266 and 1273. It is organized in a question-and-answer format.

[2] The disputed questions *On Evil*, or *Quaestiones disputatae de malo*, were probably composed in 1270.

with the Lord. A little farther on we will see the dramatic break that occurred, after Saint Thomas, between morality and spirituality, and we will see how the evolution of acedia perfectly illustrates this fracture. This is why the reassessment of acedia today could no doubt help to rediscover the fundamental unity between morality and spirituality.

The writings of Saint Thomas, therefore, are an extension of the Fathers, who were simultaneously doctors, pastors, monks, liturgists, preachers, saints, and mystics: they were all this at the same time, without separation. We will see how, under the influence of the Franciscan William of Ockham (1295–1350), people came to compartmentalize all these elements.

In order to address question 35 of the *Secunda secundae*, it is necessary to give an overview of the *Summa Theologiae*. The *Summa* was written between 1266 and 1273. The first part, the *Prima Pars*, was written in Rome between 1266 and 1268. The second part, the *Secunda Pars*, as well as the beginning of the third, the *Tertia Pars*, were composed in Paris in eighteen months—that is, in an extraordinarily short time—between 1271 and 1272. Then Saint Thomas stopped writing on December 6, 1273. By then he had reached the sacrament of penance. The rest, known by the name of *Supplement*, was composed by his disciples. We therefore have before us a *Summa* consisting of three parts, the second further subdivided into two, which finally makes four parts. The three parts appear as follows:

— *Prima Pars*: the mystery of God in himself and also the procession of creatures from God: God in his Trinity and the creatures that emerge or proceed from God. God creates human beings outside himself, but they are called to enter one day into his own life.

— *Secunda Pars*: the return of these creatures to God.

— *Tertia Pars*: the way of this return, that is, Christ. This part, which was left unfinished, was supposed to end with eternal life, eschatology.

The second part, which interests us here, is therefore itself divided into two parts, the *Prima secundae* (first part of the second part) and the *Secunda secundae* (second part of the second part). According to the modern way of thinking about moral theology, these two parts are, on the one hand, *fundamental* moral theology and, on the other hand, *special* moral theology. However, the Dominican Albert Patfoort[3] saw very clearly that this *Secunda Pars* in reality involved a more fundamental division: on the one hand, the first five questions, which concern the end, the *finis*, which is beatitude; on the other hand, all the rest, that is, the things that lead us to that end, *ea quae sunt ad finem*, therefore, what brings us to beatitude. The first five questions, then, are the goal toward which we are headed, the driving force of all human action and, at the same time, the conclusion. This strategic positioning of beatitude at the beginning and at the end of human action generates an extraordinary dynamism in the thought of Saint Thomas.

Once we have removed these first five questions, which, in reality, are not part of the *Prima secundae* but rather precede it, the remaining text is subdivided into two:

---

[3] See A. Patfoort, *La Somme de saint Thomas et la logique du dessein de Dieu* (Paris: Parole et Silence, 1998), 70.

—what is usually called *fundamental* morals, in other words, human acts, the passions, then the *habitus* and the virtues, the gifts of the Holy Spirit, grace, laws, and

—what is usually called *special* moral theology, in other words, the review of each of the virtues (theological virtues, cardinal virtues, and those associated with them), with the sins opposed to them, as well as the different states of life.

The First Definition of Acedia: Sadness about Spiritual Good

All these elements must be kept in mind in order to understand correctly the first definition of acedia that Saint Thomas proposes: "sloth is sorrow for spiritual good" (*acedia est tristitia de bono divino*).[4] Saint Thomas deliberately aligns himself with Pope Saint Gregory, for whom acedia was a form of sadness. And yet, in an altogether new insight, he describes it as the first sin against the joy that springs from charity. He makes it the sin against the *gaudium de caritate*. Now, as we will see, the word *gaudium* has, for Saint Thomas, a very particular technical sense. Before explaining it, we must say a few words about the way in which Saint Thomas sees the "passions". Indeed, in saying that acedia is a form of "sadness", Saint Thomas Aquinas is saying that it is a passion. Let us therefore examine the passions for a moment.

---

[4] II-II, q. 35, a. 2, corp.

The passions in Thomistic works

In speaking philosophically about a "passion", we think immediately of the opposite of an "action". Now, although an action and a passion are indeed different, it is necessary to understand clearly that the difference between an action and a passion is not the difference between a voluntary act (which would be the action) and an involuntary act (which would be the passion). In fact, Saint Thomas has already made this distinction between *voluntary act* and *involuntary act* earlier, in speaking about human acts and acts of a human being:

— a human act (*actus humanus*) is one that is deliberate, voluntary, and free.

— an act of a human being (*actus hominis*) is a non-deliberate act. For example, breathing is an act of a human being, but not a human act.

Thus the difference between an action and a passion does not coincide with the difference between a voluntary act and an involuntary act. In reality, the difference between *action* and *passion* is situated *within* the human act. Saint Thomas construes "passion" as an affective reaction, an emotion or feeling that occurs with regard to a particular evil or good. In this sense, a passion is neutral. You see how far we are from the *logismoi* we mentioned previously: Evagrius understood "passion" as something almost always negative, comparable to a demon. His ideal of life was *apathéia*: the absence of passions. According to him, only a man liberated from his (wicked) passions could finally know God. But *apathéia* is not a Thomistic ideal or even a Christian ideal. For Saint Thomas, on the contrary, a passion is that interior dynamism which enables us to act, which as such is neither good nor bad, but becomes good or bad according to the object it regards and the orientation it takes.

However, since Saint Thomas has an extremely unified concept of the human being, a passion—which is an emotion or a feeling—is not impervious to reason. In this sense, reason will be able to work through it, and the passion will truly be able to become a very powerful motive force of human action. We will return to this in our examination of the second definition of acedia that Saint Thomas gives.

It must be kept clearly in mind that, for the Ancients, morality was fundamentally a response to the question of happiness. Think of the encounter of Jesus with the rich young man: "Teacher, what good deed must I do, to have eternal life?" (Mt 19:16). Man was created with a view to an end, which is happiness. Now the first experience that a man has of happiness is *pleasure*. Saint Thomas reflects therefore on the passions as the initial experiences of happiness. And among all these passions, there is one that is fundamental, and that is *love*. Saint Thomas tells us, in question 28 of the *Prima secundae*, that "every agent, whatever it be, does every action from love of some kind."[5] And this is always true. Even if he does something bad, man does it out of a certain love (*ex aliquo amore*).

Let us take a little example: a child is playing with a ball in the living room while his mother is running errands. Now the ball tips over a Chinese vase that was on

---

[5] II-II, q. 28, a. 6, corp.

the mantelpiece. What will he say when his mother comes back? Faced with this delicate situation, the child has the choice between telling a lie and telling the truth. But if he chooses the lie, by saying for instance that the cat was the one that tipped over the vase (!), he does not do this out of hatred for the truth. He does it because the goods that result from the lie (maternal love, dessert, television, lack of punishment, and so on) seem to him much more concrete and much more attractive than the truth. Thus, even if he lies, the child does so "out of love" for these goods that attract him. And we could give many other examples that show how, when we do evil, it is because it always appears to us as a certain good, even if it is a false good.

Thus we see how, for Saint Thomas, man is naturally oriented toward the good, whether this good is genuine or illusory. And so when man happens to sin, he still does it *ex amore*, for love of an object that seems to him to be a good, even though it is an illusory and false good. When we study Saint Thomas, we are struck by the fact that he addresses sin only reluctantly, when he cannot do otherwise. Fundamentally, his perspective is resolutely positive. For him, every man who acts is oriented toward the good: when he does evil, it is because somehow the evil appears to him as a good. Love is therefore the motive force of our action.

The circular movement of love

In this perspective, every action can be divided into three moments, which I will first list for you:

1. The affective union or intentional union (*unio affectus*)
2. The desire (*desiderium*)
3. The real union or joy (*gaudium*)

Let us look at each of these stages in terms of an example. A young woman is at home and has to go shopping for bread. Her husband, or someone who loves her a lot, is at her side and says to her, "I will go with you." And since they are together, they do not take the usual route but walk in a roundabout way that leads them to pass in front of a jeweler's shop. Now the woman is attracted by two magnificent earrings that have just been put on display in the window. Note well that she did not go in search of jewelry. She went out to shop for bread, but, in passing, she was attracted and enthralled by the jewels. This is precisely the first moment of the action, what we call the *affective* or *intentional union* (*unio affectus*), which in turn is subdivided into three smaller moments:

a. the *immutatio* (change): the woman is passive initially; the earrings are what have an impact on her and will lead her to change;

b. the *coaptatio* (adaptation): the earrings have touched, transformed the young woman and have adapted her to themselves;

c. the *complacentia* (complaisance): the young woman, who for the moment only tends toward union with the object, nevertheless already rejoices in thinking about that object. She is already in relation with that object; she already has a certain complaisance in it, a certain union with it, a union that is called "in-tentional" because the woman "tends toward" the object that has touched her.

This is when we arrive at the second moment of the action: the desire (*desiderium*). The earrings have enkindled in the young woman's heart a deep desire, which urges her not to remain there. She then goes from passivity to activity. At this stage, the subject sets all her potency into action in order to attain the object. In our example, the force of the desire will urge the woman to pursue the object, by reminding her husband, for example, that it will soon be their anniversary. Finally, they will enter the shop and buy the pair of earrings. There is an intense dynamism in the movement of desire, but you see, too, how *love* precedes *desire*.

Finally, we arrive at the third moment of the action: the husband pays for the earrings, and the young woman puts them on. This is the joy, *gaudium*. This is the real union with the object. She is not simply tending toward the object, she has truly attained it.

Based on this little example, we have just seen that there is a *circular movement* in love. And this is always true: every action can always be divided into these three moments. This is true for every *object*—since the word "object" is to be understood here in the sense of "what is facing the subject". I took a trivial example, but one could take an example of human love, of friendship. For example, I do not look in the telephone book in order to decide what person I will love. I meet that person, and there is then a moment of passivity, of gratuitousness, during which the person touches me, has an impact on me, and changes me in the depths of my soul, to the point where I desire to have a deeper relationship with that person, to enter into communion with her.

What we have just said about human love or friendship is true also about God. Saint John tells us, in his First Letter, what charity consists of: "not that we loved God, but that he loved us" (1 Jn 4:10). God is the one who adapted us to himself, so that we might one day become sharers in the very nature of God. This is the level at which the joy of charity will be found, the *gaudium de caritate* that we will discuss shortly.

Thus, love is at the root of action. And love, at its own root, involves a moment of passivity. It is, so to speak, awakened by an encounter, which already happens to be a promise of accomplishment. And this encounter engenders a certain intentional presence, which proves to be the stimulus for the whole spiritual life, so as to attain a genuine presence, a veritable communion.

There are therefore three moments in our action, which can be assumed directly from a spiritual perspective: presence, encounter, communion.

The joy that springs from charity

At the conclusion of the circular movement that I have just explained, there is joy (*gaudium*), which Saint Thomas takes pains to distinguish from pleasure (*delectatio*). *Delectatio* is the rather corporeal and natural pleasure, and *gaudium* is the joy that is spiritual, in which reason has its own place.

We have to say a word about this altogether special *gaudium* which is the *gaudium* of charity. Saint Thomas is the first to consider charity to be a sort of *friendship*. In the history of philosophy, friendship was always considered a value, but Saint Thomas is the first to make charity a kind of friendship. In order to reach this conclusion that charity is indeed a form of friendship, he takes pains to reason very rigorously. He asks himself what are the characteristics of friendship. He discovers three of them:

1. First of all, it is a love of *benevolence*. In this regard, it is necessary to recall the classic distinction between two sorts of love: the love of concupiscence or of desire, which is self-directed (*amor concupiscentiae*), and the love of benevolence or of friendship, which is directed toward the other (*amor benevolentiae*).

2. Furthermore, reciprocity is necessary: this is the *mutua amatio*. I can love someone, but if that person does not love me in return, he is not truly my friend, and there is no real friendship.

3. Finally, there has to be something in common between the two friends: this is the *communicatio*.

Having thus defined friendship, Saint Thomas asks himself whether such a relationship is possible between God and man. He therefore examines the three essential characteristics of friendship and inquires whether they are present in the relationship between God and man.

As far as the first characteristic is concerned, the *love of benevolence*, the answer is simple enough: God, quite obviously, loves me with a love of benevolence. For man's part, the individual is divided between the love of God for his own sake and the love of God for what he has promised me

—namely, participation in divine life—but there is nevertheless a love that is truly a love of benevolence. The first requirement is therefore fulfilled.

As for the second characteristic, *reciprocity*, the answer is likewise rather simple: God loves me, and I love him. The second requirement is therefore fulfilled.

In contrast, as far as the third characteristic is concerned, the *things in common*, the answer is more difficult. Indeed, it seems that there is absolutely nothing in common between God and man. The abyss between human nature and divine nature is infinite. Nevertheless, Saint Thomas answers that there is indeed something in common between God and man. And this is *beatitude*. God willed that the *communicatio*, the thing in common between him and man, should be beatitude, in other words, participation in his own life.

Those who still consider Saint Thomas Aquinas a dry, cold, and unspiritual man ought to change their opinion! Indeed, there is nothing more expansive and exalting than this perspective of charity understood as a form of friendship.

Having reached this point in his presentation, Saint Thomas Aquinas cites Aristotle, in the *Nicomachean Ethics*. In this passage, Aristotle writes: "For what we do by means of our friends, is done, in a sense, by ourselves."[6] In other words, if I cannot do something, but my friend does it, then it is somehow as though I was the one who did it. Saint

---

[6] Aristotle, *Nicomachean Ethics*, bk. III, 3 as cited from a Latin translation in I-II, q. 5, a. 5, ad 1. As translated from the Greek in *Ethica Nicomachea*, vol. 9 of *The Works of Aristotle*, ed. David Ross, 6th ed. (1915; Oxford: Clarendon Press, 1966), 1112b, ll. 25–28: "Things that might be brought about by our own efforts . . . in a sense include things that can be brought about by the efforts of our friends, since the moving principle is in ourselves."

Thomas repeats this idea and applies it to the friendship with God: what man cannot do alone, namely, attain the ultimate end that consists in the vision of God, man can do through his friendship with God, by means of charity. Here the friend is the divine friend, the Beloved with a capital B; it is God himself.

This *gaudium de caritate* is the joy that springs from friendship with God and from this interpersonal communion, the fundamental object of which is beatitude, participation in God's life, which is already anticipated here below through grace.

We can therefore distinguish two joys of charity:

—the ultimate joy when, in eternal life, we will participate definitively in the very life of God: we will be God through participation, and,

—here below, the joy that springs from our life with God through grace, the sacraments, prayer, and the life of faith.

Having seen what this *gaudium de caritate* is, it becomes possible to perceive what the specific *sadness* of acedia is. The passion of sadness, for Saint Thomas, is precisely the opposite of the passion of joy. Whereas joy is at the terminus of the movement of love, sadness is at the terminus of the movement of hatred. And whereas joy is a certain *delectatio*, a certain pleasure, so too sadness is a certain *dolor*, a certain sorrow. Whereas joy is an affective reaction to a present good, sadness is an affective reaction to a present evil. In the case of acedia, what is this evil? Saint Thomas answers: It is spiritual good, the *bonum divinum*. But how is it possible that man should be saddened by the prospect of spiritual good, as though that spiritual good were an evil? Acedia is like that, however, and we immediately perceive the gravity of it: acedia is a kind of sadness when faced with spiritual good, which appears to man to be an evil.

In the *Summa Theologiae*, Saint Thomas does not explain how man can come to be sad about what is nevertheless his ultimate good. But in his treatise *De malo*, he poses the question frankly: If it is quite logical that every agent should act first out of love, then how is it that man can be saddened in the presence of God? And Thomas answers: Man is capable of being sad in the presence of God because for God's sake he must renounce other goods that are carnal, temporal, limited, apparent goods, which on the scale, though, will weigh more than spiritual good, which may seem much less concrete than some particular good that is immediately attainable.[7]

When Saint Thomas describes acedia as a sin against the *gaudium de caritate*, this whole argument is in the background. Saint Thomas situates acedia at the terminus of the circular movement of the love of friendship that exists between God and us: acedia makes us sad about what ought to be, however, our greatest joy, namely, sharing in the life of God, by grace here below and by the beatific vision in eternal life. But let us not forget that the beatific vision is an act of communion. When Saint Thomas tells

[7] Cf. *De malo*, q. 11, a. 1 and 2.

us, in question 3 of the *Secunda Pars*, that beatitude is an act of the *speculative intellect*, we must remember that the word "speculative" is practically synonymous with "contemplative" and therefore suggests communion, "knowledge" in the biblical sense of that term. All this is quite traditional. Gregory of Nyssa has already said: "The true sight of God consists in this, that the one who looks up to God never ceases in that desire."[8]

Thus the first definition of acedia given by Saint Thomas presents it as a *sadness about God*. We understand, henceforth, how it affects man's relationship with God. Acedia causes sadness, a negative reaction to what ought to be our greatest happiness, participation in the life of God. You can already see how far removed from Saint Thomas was the nineteenth-century view of acedia merely as a distraction in prayer or negligence in some particular pious exercise.

Now we must look at the second definition that Saint Thomas gives of acedia, namely, disgust with activity, *taedium operandi*. We will speak about human acts in their dynamic tendency toward beatitude. We will find charity again, this time not as friendship but, rather, as a good *habitus*, in other words, as a virtue that, being present at the heart of every action, helps us to make it attain its true end, which is union with God. Acedia as disgust with that action will then appear to be the risk of paralysis of the spiritual and supernatural movement whereby, even within our act, we can fully participate in the divine life. After that we will consider the remedy that Saint Thomas proposes to us in our battle against acedia.

[8] Gregory of Nyssa, *The Life of Moses* 233 (Mahwah, N.J.: Paulist Press, 1978), 115.

The Second Definition of Acedia: Disgust with Activity

I have tried to show that behind the definition of acedia as "sadness about spiritual good" there was a whole affective movement, in the sense that Saint Thomas gives to the word *affectus*, namely, a movement that reaches being itself and, in the final analysis, a spiritual movement of man as he journeys toward participation in the very life of God. Herein resides fundamentally the joy of man, even now by grace and one day completely in beatitude. Thus we see the gravity of acedia, which is opposed to this joy of participating in God's life.

We must now examine the second definition of acedia that Saint Thomas gives: the famous *taedium operandi* or "disgust with activity". Acedia, according to this definition, appears no longer to be a sadness about God but, rather, to be a sluggishness that prevents one from acting, which prevents one from bringing the act to its fulfillment. This definition of acedia is extremely important, because it offers us an interpretive key to all moral theology.

In order to understand the expression *taedium operandi* correctly, we must situate it within a larger perspective, as we did with the first definition. We have already spoken earlier about beatitude, but we must return to the topic now. As we have already noted, Saint Thomas Aquinas devotes the first five questions of the second part of his *Summa Theologiae* to beatitude.

He starts by making a distinction between two elements of beatitude: the *finis cujus* (the object itself of beatitude) and the *finis quo* (the act by which a soul will be blessed). Of course, as Thomas himself explains, there is no reason to separate these two aspects. Indeed, the object of beatitude is attained by the very act that makes us blessed. However, in making this distinction between beatitude as participation in the life of God and the beatifying act, Saint Thomas does show that beatitude is an act, an activity, contrary to a common representation of eternal life that conceives of it as static repose (*requiem aeternam*). Now the perfection of a being consists in its being *in act*, because potency without act remains imperfect. In this sense, what profoundly realizes and fulfills the human person is an *operatio*, in other words, a movement into act. We see here that the morality of Saint Thomas Aquinas is more than a morality of the virtues: it is a morality of act. It is even a *morality of excellent activity*, since virtue, which is the principle of the act, has in itself a connotation of excellence: it simultaneously renders good the act and the person who places it.

What perfectly actualizes the human person is therefore a perfect act: beatitude. But this excellent, definitive activity is prepared here below by our acts. This is why Saint Thomas, immediately after the five questions devoted to beatitude, continues his *Summa Theologiae* with the study of human acts (I-II, qq. 6ff.). Our acts are like steps that either bring us closer to the vision of God or else distance us from it, depending on whether they are good or bad. We find again here the dynamic perspective of Evagrius and the whole tradition: through baptism, we left Egypt by receiving the grace of God, and we then began a *journey* through the desert, which leads us to the Promised Land. Saint Benedict and Saint John Climacus, in contrast, speak

about a *ladder* by which we ascend to the heavenly home-
land, but the idea is still the same: we advance toward a
goal. For Saint Thomas, human acts are a preparation and,
even more, an anticipation: we already see God in human
activity. We have a marvelous example of this in the lives
of the martyrs. The activity and the witness of the martyrs are already a revelation of the face of God: in their
lives we see God. There is therefore an original character
that is altogether specific to moral theology: in the activity
of man, we discover who God is. The activity of man—
particularly the activity of the saints—reveals a true reflection of God's face. There is an original character to the
lives of the saints in which the mystery of God is reflected.

Virtue is not a habit

If we consider activity as an anticipation of beatitude, we
then see how the "disgust with activity" concerns beatitude. Acedia as disgust with activity is therefore an obstacle to beatitude. However, it is necessary to go farther.
Indeed, at the heart of activity there is a virtue: charity.
We have already spoken about charity from a very particular point of view: the perspective of charity as friendship. We address it here as a virtue. But, then, what is a
virtue? Saint Thomas Aquinas defines it quite simply as a
habitus. Be careful, though: *habitus* is not a "habit"! I refer
you here to the magisterial article by Father Servais Pinckaers, O.P., which has become a landmark study: "Virtue Is Quite Different from a Habit."[9] The only point of

---

[9] Servais Pinckaers, "La vertu est tout autre chose qu'une habitude", *NRT*
(1960): 387–403, reprinted in *Le renouveau de la morale: Études pour une morale*

similarity between a virtue and a habit is the fact that both are acquired by the repetition of acts, but even this similarity is not total, since virtue involves the repetition of interior acts and not just of exterior acts, as is the case with habit. A century after Aquinas, William of Ockham, identifying virtue with habit, would opine that virtue is an obstacle to human freedom. Of course, if you are shaped by habits, you lose part of your freedom; but, strictly speaking, virtue is not a habit. It is an extraordinary inventive capacity that enables us to carry out excellent acts that are profoundly in conformity with God's will. It is a stable disposition to do good.

Let us go into more detail. A virtue has three characteristics:

1. First of all, it is an *operative habitus*, in other words, an operative disposition that enables us to *act*; it is a capacity that continually perfects our activity.

2. It is also an *elective habitus*, in other words, it impels us to *choose*. Saint Thomas Aquinas gives a very detailed description of the different parts of the human act: there are twelve of them, and the last part of this human act, which in the end sums up the other eleven, is *choice*.

3. There is, finally, a *good* elective operative *habitus*. It is good not only because the virtue enables us to choose the good, but also because it makes the acting subject good. It influences the subject: when I act rightly, I become good.

fidèle à ses sources et à sa mission présente, Cahiers de l'Actualité Religieuse 19 (Tournay: Casterman, 1964).

In order to acquire these virtues, we need an *education*. When a baby starts to crawl on all fours in the house, his father teaches him not to put his fingers into the electrical outlets. This establishes a law. When the child is faced with this prohibition, there is a danger that he will take it as a restriction of his freedom. It is a bit like what happened in the Garden of Eden: "If you eat the fruit of that tree, you shall die" (cf. Gen 2:17). This is not about a jealous God who fears that man might become his equal. On the contrary, it is about an excellent father who says: "My child, do not eat that, or it will harm you." The day will come when the child understands that the prohibition was established for his own good. At the beginning, the law is necessary, not to crush our freedom, but to protect us. The law is a schoolmaster who is there to help us. When virtue has become more firmly rooted in us, we no longer need the law; we can act easily and joyously in the Good.

We often have an erroneous concept of freedom. We think that freedom is the ability to choose between contraries and, therefore, the possibility of choosing evil. We think that a transgression is a manifestation of our freedom. But that is not true at all. Let us take a musical comparison: the violinist who practices his exercises for hours acquires little by little a greater mastery of his instrument. Will he be less free as a result? Would freedom be, for him, the ability to play wrong notes? Is it not instead such mastery of his instrument that if, unfortunately, a string were to slacken during a concert, he could continue to play without anyone noticing the problem? Virtue is precisely what enables us to perform excellent actions easily and joyfully, in a stable manner, with profound interior freedom, the freedom of the children of God.

Charity, the most eminent of the virtues

It is customary to distinguish between the theological virtues and the moral virtues. The *theological* virtues are so called because they refer directly to God: they have God as their origin, their motive, and their object. They are faith, hope, and charity. The *moral* virtues are the other virtues, which are acquired in a human manner. They are rooted in the theological virtues, which animate and enliven them. Among the moral virtues there are four that play a pivotal role. This is why they are called the *cardinal* virtues (from the Latin *cardo*, hinge), because all the other virtues are grouped around them. They are prudence, justice, fortitude, and temperance.

Having thus explained what the virtues are, let us dwell on the most eminent among them, charity. Charity is indeed the most eminent of the virtues, because it is, in us, the principle of our most perfect activity: uniting ourselves with God in love and conforming ourselves to him. Saint Thomas says that charity is the *form* of the other virtues, in other words, it orients the virtues, along with the acts of those virtues, toward the true end, which is participation in the love of God. Charity is at the heart of human action. In fact, charity is not only the greatest love of which we are capable. It is also—and above all—a gift from God. It is the participation of the Holy Spirit. It is therefore not only our most eminent love; it is of a different order.

This opens up a whole new vista in which we can talk

about the Holy Spirit at the heart of our activity. In the moral part of the *Catechism of the Catholic Church*, we find two expressions that describe the moral life: "life in Christ" and "life in the Spirit". The latter expression is very important. Indeed, charity is a gratuitous gift, it is the participation of the Holy Spirit, according to the verse from the Letter of Saint Paul to the Romans: "God's love has been poured into our hearts through the Holy Spirit who has been given to us" (Rom 5:5). There is, then, a close connection between our moral life and the grace of God. Commentators have remarked that the word most often used by Saint Thomas Aquinas when he speaks about the Holy Spirit is the word "movement" (*motus*, which can also be translated as "prompting"). In this sense, all our activity can be considered life under the influence of the Holy Spirit.

However, it is important to understand correctly the nature of this "influence", of this movement. Indeed, we are not moved *externally*, as is the case with a drunk who staggers along and must be guided by tapping alternately on his right shoulder and his left shoulder, so that he walks more or less straight ahead. No, the Holy Spirit moves us *from within*, while deeply respecting our temperament, our character, what we are. Charity is the mother and the form of the virtues, in the sense that it conceives and commands the acts of the other virtues, while deeply respecting the specificity of each virtue. Similarly, charity is found at the heart of our activity, allowing our acts, even the simplest ones, to attain their true end, while deeply respecting what each one of us is. The Holy Spirit moves us from within, so that each of our potentialities might produce its own effect. Charity and the Holy Spirit, however, never impede our freedom. This is the mystery of freedom and grace. Our everyday activity, even the most trivial, can be transformed by the Holy Spirit and attain its ultimate end, which is participation in the life of God.

Acedia, sin against charity at the very heart of activity

It is understandable, then, that the two definitions of acedia converge. In effect, acedia is a sin against charity in two ways, which meet in reality. On the one hand, acedia is a sin against the joy that springs from charity; it is sadness about what ought to gladden us most: participation in the very life of God. On the other hand, acedia is a sin against charity when it crushes or paralyzes activity, because then it affects the deepest motive force of activity, namely, charity, the participation of the Holy Spirit.

Acedia is therefore a sin against charity in our spiritual dimension of union with God, of interpersonal communion with the Lord; but it is also a sin against charity at the very heart of our activity, by preventing our activity from attaining its ultimate end. Herein lies its truly formidable character. You see how far removed this is from the romantic notion that acedia is feeling blue, a sort of melancholy or depression. This is why some have said that acedia was a "theological" vice, in the sense that it truly affects the very life of God in us, our deepest way of relating to God.

In this second definition of acedia, Saint Thomas uses the expression "disgust with activity" (*taedium operandi*). He found the word *taedium* in the writings of Cassian:

this word designates a certain disgust, spiritual disgust. By adding the gerund *operandi*, Saint Thomas indicates that this disgust concerns the dynamism of action: it is, so to speak, a break in the impetus, a paralysis, a halt that cuts us off from God. Acedia is therefore not an external obstacle; it is an *interior* obstacle. In this sense, acedia can even be a mortal sin, that is, a sin that turns man away from God and destroys charity in his soul, since it can cut man off from God at the very heart of his activity.

The Daughters of Acedia

As he does for each of the seven capital sins, Saint Thomas, following Cassian, assigns offspring to acedia, in other words, sins that depend on it. Now he divides these sins into two categories:

— on the one hand, the sins whereby we *flee the acts that sadden us*;
— on the other hand, the sins whereby we *seek compensations*.

1. In the first category, we can again make two subdivisions. Indeed, one can flee the things that sadden us in two ways:

— either by *avoidance*
— or else by *struggling*.

   a. Now there are three sins that spring from acedia through *avoidance*:

—One can flee the end itself—beatitude—which appears to us as a form of sadness. This, then, is *despair*, the first and most terrible daughter of acedia. Saint Thomas minces things even more finely. He says that someone can flee beatitude in two ways, either because he has a certain disgust with the things of God (*fastidium*) or else, more subtly, because he thinks that beatitude is very good but that he is unworthy of it, that it is good for everyone except himself. This is despair in the strictest sense: it is the famous sin against the Holy Spirit.

—One can also avoid the things that lead us to the end (*ea quae sunt ad finem*). Here again, one can do this in two ways:

   —either these acts that lead us to the end are advisable but difficult, for example, the evangelical counsels. In this case, we have *faint-heartedness*, a lack of courage.

   —or else these acts that lead us to beatitude are prescribed. In this case we have *torpor with regard to the commandments*.

b. There are also two sins that spring from acedia by *struggling* against what saddens us:

—this may be a sort of struggling against persons, which is *rancor*;

—or it may be a sort of struggling against the spiritual goods themselves: this is *malice*. One then ends up hating the good.

2. The second category, that is, the search for compensations, involves what Saint Thomas calls "wandering after unlawful things". He gives details about this wandering by dividing it into five possibilities:

— *uneasiness of the mind*
— *curiosity*
— *loquacity*
— *restlessness of the body*
— *instability*

You see, therefore, the complex variety of forms that acedia can assume. When he discusses the seriousness of these different forms of acedia, Saint Thomas observes that the most serious form is to despair of beatitude: someone thinks that God cannot give him beatitude because he is not worthy of his mercy. This rejection of divine mercy is, properly speaking, the sin against the Holy Spirit; Jesus tells us that there is no remission for this sin. This calls to mind, of course, the last "Instrument of Good Works" listed in the *Rule of Saint Benedict*: "never to despair of God's mercy" (*RB* 4, 72). Of all these instruments of the spiritual art that Benedict recommends, he concludes with the one that must not be abandoned in any circumstances. If it were necessary to keep only one, he seems to tell us, let it be that one!

The Definitive Remedy for Acedia

Given the extreme seriousness of acedia, a terrible obstacle to life with God, Saint Thomas proposes for us a remedy.

Now this remedy has a peculiar characteristic: it is definitive! Thomas speaks about it, not in the *Summa Theologiae*,
but in another work, the *Summa contra Gentiles* (that is, the
summa against the "pagans"), which was composed several years before the *Summa Theologiae*. We find this passage in chapter 54 of book 4. There Thomas inquires into
the reasons for the appropriateness of the Incarnation, in
other words, into the reasons why God became man. In
the *Summa Theologiae*, Saint Thomas would again address
the question and would say that God became incarnate essentially to save mankind from sin. Thereby the aspect of
redemption is highlighted. In the *Summa contra Gentiles*, in
contrast, priority is given instead to the aspect of *diviniza-
tion*: God became man so that man might participate in
the divine life, so that he might himself become God by
participation.

Here are a few excerpts from this very beautiful passage:

> First, then, let this be taken into consideration: The Incar-
> nation of God was the most efficacious assistance to man
> in his striving for beatitude. For we have shown in Book
> III that the perfect beatitude of man consists in the imme-
> diate vision of God. It might, of course, appear to some
> that man would never have the ability to achieve this state:
> that the human intellect be united immediately to the di-
> vine essence itself as an intellect is to its intelligible; for
> there is an unmeasured distance between the natures.[10]

In other words, it might seem impossible, given the infinite distance between the nature of man and the nature

[10] Thomas Aquinas, *On the Truth of the Catholic Faith: Summa contra Gentiles*,
bk. 4: *Salvation*, trans. Charles J. O'Neil (Garden City, N.Y.: Image Books,
1957), chap. 54, p. 228.

of God, that man could one day share the very life of God. Saint Thomas continues:

> Thus, in the search for beatitude, a man would grow cold, held back by very desperation [acedia]. But the fact that God was willing to unite human nature to Himself personally points out to men with greatest clarity that man can be united to God by intellect, and see Him immediately.[11]

The extraordinary remedy for acedia is therefore the Incarnation! Given the abyss that separates divine nature and human nature, God built a bridge, which is his own Son, the High Priest, literally "the bridge-maker" (*pontifex*). We find here, once again, an image that is very dear to Saint Benedict. In chapter 27 of his *Rule*, Benedict speaks about the abbot's solicitude for the brothers who have committed grave sins. In this chapter, Benedict describes the abbot by using two images: the abbot as physician and the abbot as pastor. These two images, moreover, converge, since the pastor ends up becoming a physician for his sheep. This is the chapter where Saint Benedict speaks also about the parable of the lost sheep.

The patristic tradition saw in this parable an image of the Incarnation. Leaving on the mountain the ninety-nine sheep, that is, the angels in heaven, God set out in search of the lost sheep, humanity. After reaching the place where it was, in the brambles and the mud of its sin, God put it on his shoulders; he put on the human condition. In this way he was able to bring it back to the flock, in other words, to the Father's house. In Ravenna there is a magnificent

[11] Ibid.

mosaic dedicated to this theme in the apse of the Basilica of Saint Apollinaris *in Classe*: it depicts the bishop, Saint Apollinaris, surrounded with ninety-nine stars, which symbolize the ninety-nine sheep. On his shoulders there is a *pallium*, the sign of his episcopal dignity, which is made out of the wool of the sheep. This pallium symbolizes the lost sheep that he carries on his shoulders, in imitation of Christ, so as to bring it back to the sheepfold.

In describing the Incarnation as the definitive remedy for acedia, Saint Thomas asserts that from now on the distance between human nature and divine nature is overcome by the Son of God himself. Fully God and fully man, Christ restores to us the hope of being able to participate fully in the divine life; he reopens for us the path to beatitude.

A little farther on, Saint Thomas makes a second argument:

> But man was able to be misled into this clinging as [though] to an end to things [that are] less than God in existence by his ignorance of the worthiness of his nature. Thus it happens with some. They look on themselves in their bodily and sentient nature—which they have in common with other animals—and in bodily things and fleshly pleasures they seek out a kind of animal beatitude.[12]

Indeed, what happens when man despairs of attaining heavenly beatitude? He runs the risk of degrading the object of his desire, the object of his happiness, contenting himself then with what Saint Thomas calls an "animal beatitude". When the desired object totally exceeds the capacities of the subject, he is in fact tempted to be con-

[12] Ibid., 228–29.

tent with desiring a more immediately accessible object. In this case, the Incarnation comes to restore to man the possibility, once again, of walking toward true beatitude. The Incarnation thus allows man to rediscover his proper dignity.

Saint Thomas proposes yet a third reason for the appropriateness of the Incarnation, namely: to lead man to love his God better. Here is what he writes:

> The desire to enjoy anything is caused by love of that thing. Therefore, man, tending to perfect beatitude, needed inducement to the divine love. Nothing, of course, so induces us to love [some]one as the experience of his love for us. But God's love for men could be demonstrated to man in no way more effective than this: He willed to be united to man in person, for it is proper to love to unite the lover with the beloved as far as possible.[13]

God therefore manifested to us his love by becoming man. Henceforth we have, as it were, the "proof" that he loves us and is inviting us to share his own life. We are therefore delivered from acedia and from the despair that it engenders. In becoming man, God became our friend and therefore can love us as a friend loves his friend.

These three reasons of appropriateness for the Incarnation should fill us with joy. From now on we are saved from acedia, because Christ has delivered us once for all from sin and from the resulting despair. The Incarnation is therefore the definitive remedy for acedia: it truly restores to us the joy of being saved. Does this mean that nothing remains for us to do? Not at all! What remains for us is to

[13] Ibid., 230–31.

receive this salvation. This is precisely what Catholic doctrine calls "merit". Let us look at a little example, inspired by Saint Thomas.

Imagine a small child standing beside a very tall piece of furniture, a mantelpiece, for example. On top of that mantelpiece there is an excellent remedy that will cure him of all his ills, present or future. Alas, this remedy is totally beyond the child's reach. Despite all his efforts, he will never be able to get to it. His mother, who loves her child very much, wants to give him this remedy, because she knows that it is good for him.

The mother has two options: either she takes the remedy on the mantelpiece and gives it to the child; or else she takes the child into her arms, so that the child can take the remedy himself. The first option shows much love: the mother offers to her child something that he could never have without her. But the second option shows even more love: indeed, the mother allows her child to reach by himself for what she, in reality, is giving him quite gratuitously.

Now, Saint Thomas tells us, this is precisely what God does with regard to us. God, by his excess of love, wants us to participate and to obtain by ourselves, up to a certain point, what in fact he gives us absolutely gratuitously. God calls us to collaborate in his work of salvation. God does not save us without us.

Saint Thérèse of the Child Jesus had understood this perfectly when she related, in her autobiographical *Story of a Soul*, that one day, as she stood at the foot of a stairway and tried to put her little foot on the first step, she kept falling. Then her mother, hearing this, came over to her, took her in her arms, and carried her up the stairs. And Thérèse adds:

> We are living now in an age of inventions, and we no longer have to take the trouble of climbing stairs, for, in the homes of the rich, an elevator has replaced these very successfully. . . . The elevator which must raise me to heaven is Your arms, O Jesus![14]

Thérèse had understood perfectly that God, out of an excess of love, wants us to collaborate in his work of salvation. Left to our own devices, we can do nothing. But if we do everything that we can, God will catch hold of us and will himself lead us to beatitude.

Summary of the Thought of Saint Thomas Aquinas on Acedia

Before speaking about commentary on acedia and, more generally, about moral theology and Christian action in the centuries that followed Saint Thomas Aquinas, I would like to summarize briefly what we have seen thus far.

A. As a preliminary, I will restate the teaching in the writings of Saint Thomas about the circular movement of love. Saint Thomas' profound insight is that we always act out of love, by being drawn, by attraction to the Good. This is the way of acting freely: acting because of a stable, joyous

---

[14] *Story of a Soul: The Autobiography of St. Thérèse of Lisieux*, study edition, trans. John Clarke, O.C.D. (Washington, D.C.: ICS Publications, 2005), 10.

attraction to the Good. In every action we can distinguish three moments that form a circular movement:

1. The first moment is the impact produced on us by an object (see the story about the jewelry). This object touches the subject in a moment of passivity, in an amazing, unexpected, gratuitous encounter. This first moment, which Saint Thomas calls *love*, is already a relationship, a union with the object. The subject is united to the object, not really, but "intentionally", by tending toward it. This is an *intentional* (or affective) *union*, a *unio affectus*.

2. This object impels us to adapt to it, so as to come together with it in a union that will no longer be intentional but real. This is the second moment, the moment of *desire*, a moment of activity. With all our potencies we come together with the object.

3. The third moment is the moment of *real union* with the object: *unio realis* or *gaudium*, spiritual joy.

With regard to this movement, we can speak about "circularity", because the object is at the outset of the movement, as something gratuitously offered, but also at the conclusion of the movement, which really and definitively leads to it.

B. Having explained this concept, I offer several basic points in summary:

1. Confronted with the grandeur of his vocation, man runs the risk of falling into despair and of never being

able to accomplish it. He is in danger of becoming self-centered instead of being open to the total gift of himself, in which he fulfills himself as a person. From this perspective, the Incarnation of the Son of God is like a new principle of action that delivers us from "disgust with action" and enables us to be open to the gift of divine friendship. Christ is then the way to the Father.

2. In trying to lower the object of his happiness, man runs the risk of being content with what Saint Thomas calls an "animal beatitude", in other words, a beatitude that is immediately attainable. In this sense, the Incarnation revives man's hope by making him rediscover his dignity. Thus delivered from acedia, man can experience even here below a foretaste (*praelibatio*) of beatitude, by means of faith, that savory knowledge of the mystery. Saint Thomas insists on this: thanks to the Incarnation, knowledge of the mystery is given to us in a manner that is human (*secundum modum humanum*) and no longer simply divine.

3. Since man is called to participate in the very life of God, he needs a special disposition of his affective faculties so as to be able to attain such a fullness. The Incarnation, which manifests in an unsurpassable way the original gift of God's love for man, makes possible this intentional union with God that is at the start of the circular movement of the love between God and us, which ultimately enables us to enter into an intimate relationship with the Lord, a relationship with God that is more familiar (*familiarior*). At the second stage of the movement, the stage of desire, man goes toward God with

all his affective dynamisms, all his humanity, in a profoundly incarnate way.

4. This is where the unique moment of the *encounter with Christ* occurs. God's call comes first, and it is gratuitous. He is the one who has this impact on us. We are passive in the first moment. The important thing is "not that we loved God but that he loved us", Saint John writes (1 Jn 4:10). God's call in Christ elicits from us a response that is manifested, precisely, in an action. This action is conversion to Christ. This is how Christ becomes present at the heart of each of our acts, thanks to the gift of the Holy Spirit. Here, acting in Christ and acting in the Spirit are one and become the very definition of Christian activity, of sanctity. The great encyclical of John Paul II on morality, *Veritatis splendor*, starts with a commentary on the episode of Jesus' encounter with the rich young man. John Paul II did not choose this passage at random. Indeed, the encounter with Christ is what raises the fundamental question that is at the heart of Christian morality: "How must I act in order to have eternal life?" In the works of William of Ockham, as we will see shortly, there is no longer any connection between eternal life and what we are called to do. Every act becomes separate, atomized, and thus we lose the long-term purpose. Chapter 2 of *Veritatis splendor* criticizes theological positions that lose the connection between eternal life and the concrete acts that are performed.

We said that acedia could be called a "theological" vice, in the sense that it directly affects our relationship to God.

But we can also ask to which theological virtue in particular it is opposed: faith, hope, or charity? We will see that it is opposed to all three.

First of all, acedia is opposed to *faith* inasmuch as it is a lack of confidence in man's abilities to succeed, with God's grace, in his vocation as a son in the Son. It is also a lack of faith through a lack of fidelity. Here is where the Incarnation of Christ delivers those afflicted with acedia from that infidelity, from that spiritual disgust. Acedia therefore offends against faith at the first moment of the circular movement of love, at the moment of intentional union with God.

But acedia is also opposed to *hope* in the second moment of the movement of love, the moment of desire. Acedia is opposed to *desiderium*. It engenders despair; it causes a person to flee from beatitude; it crushes the impetus of our desire. It disdains mercy. Here, the Incarnation restores to us the hope of participating one day, by a sheer gratuitous gift, in the very life of God.

Finally, acedia is opposed to *charity* in the third moment of this movement, which is real union with the loved object. Acedia is opposed to *gaudium*, to the joy of charity. But there is more: man is called to a communion of persons that is brought about in the gift of self and welcoming openness to the other. Here the Incarnation of the Son shows us, in an unsurpassable way, how a person is actualized in the gift of himself: Christ gave himself, surrendered himself, even to the point of his sacrifice on the Cross and his Eucharistic offering. He took sin upon himself; he himself became "sin", according to the daring expression of Saint Paul (2 Cor 5:21). He delivered us definitively from acedia. Here, acedia impairs charity at the very heart of our activity, not from outside, but from within. In order to conquer acedia, man is aided by a gift of the Holy Spirit: the gift of *wisdom*, which etymologically means "savory science" (*sapida scientia*). The gift of wisdom corresponds to the virtue of charity, and acedia is opposed to the gift of wisdom, but it is not victorious. Wisdom develops in us the instinct of the Holy Spirit, who directs us interiorly.

We should reread here the beautiful commentary of Saint Thomas on verse 14 of chapter 8 of the Letter to the Romans. The Latin text that Saint Thomas had before him said this, literally: "Those who are acted upon or driven (*aguntur*) by the Spirit of God, they are the children of God." Saint Thomas is interested in the passive verb *aguntur*. Who are those who "are driven", he asks? He answers: Animals are driven or moved by their instincts. They are hungry, and they eat. They are thirsty, and they drink. They have an urge to reproduce, and they reproduce. Man, on the contrary, having been created in the image and likeness of God, is master of his acts. Therefore men *agunt* (the same Latin verb in the active voice); they act. But the saints, spiritual men and women, although they act (*agunt*) as human beings, are once again acted upon or driven (*aguntur*), this time no longer by an instinct that is carnal, but rather by the instinct of the Holy Spirit (*instinctus Spiritus Sancti*). He configures us to the Son, so that we might be children of God in the Son. Our whole moral life is therefore allowing ourselves to be acted upon by the Spirit. And the gift of wisdom is what helps us to do this, by giving us a "connaturality" with the good that enables us to perceive things as God perceives them. Is that not magnificent?

Saint Thomas emphasizes here in particular the virtue of *prudence*. Prudence is the virtue of practical reason that enables man, in all circumstances, to choose what is most in conformity with the good, with his good, in such a way that his action might be excellent, without limit to the excellence, which ever increases according to God's plan for him. Here we are not in the modern mind-set of law and conscience, in which conscience is content to apply a general law to a particular case. We find instead a creative approach in which personal initiative is absolutely free. This is life in the Spirit. Moreover, there is a beatitude that accompanies this virtue: the seventh beatitude of the peacemakers, who will be called children of God (cf. Mt 5:9).

Acedia is therefore the major obstacle to the reception of God's gratuitous gift and to the accomplishment of the divine plan in Jesus Christ. In contrast, the encounter with Christ becomes a friendship that delivers us from self-centeredness. The Holy Spirit makes Christ the contemporary of every man and makes each of us another Christ. He makes our action the privileged place of our encounter with the Lord and of the construction of our true and deepest being.

Having said that, we may ask: How can it be that acedia disappeared totally from the theological and moral vocabulary? How can it be that no one speaks about it any more? This is what we must examine now.

The "Revolution" of William of Ockham
and the Disappearance of Acedia

It can be said that Blessed John Duns Scotus (1265–1308) was the one who initiated the profoundly unsettling development that would affect moral theology after Saint Thomas. However, with the arrival of the Franciscan friar William of Ockham (1300–1350) we can truly speak about a "revolution". Contradicting Saint Thomas of Aquinas, Ockham elaborated a new concept of freedom, which he called "the liberty of indifference" (*libertas indifferentiae*). Why this expression? Because, in his view, man is totally indeterminate, totally indifferent, with regard to good or evil.

It is necessary to realize that this concept is so engrained in us today that it is difficult for us to picture freedom as anything other than the possibility to choose between contrary things. However, this new concept elaborated by Ockham is a veritable revolution with respect to the classical concept of freedom. For the philosophers of Antiquity, and for the whole Christian tradition, freedom is the ability that man has—an ability belonging jointly to his intellect and will—to perform virtuous actions, good actions, excellent actions, perfect actions, when he wants and as he wants. Man's freedom is therefore his capacity to accomplish good acts easily, joyously, and lastingly. This freedom is defined by the attraction of the good.

William of Ockham, in contrast, makes freedom a moment "prior" to intellect and will. In Ockham's writings, the word "freedom" is almost synonymous with "will". Man is no longer attracted at all by the good. He finds himself in a state of total indifference with regard to good and evil. In order for him to be able to choose between good and evil, therefore, the intervention of an external element will be necessary, which Ockham identifies with the *law*. From then on, according to this concept, obedience to the law is what defines the good: "It is good because the law requires it of me", instead of "The law requires it of me because it is good." This is a veritable "revolution", which will eventually lead to what would be called "legalism", whereby the law alone is the criterion of the good. Today we can observe the havoc caused by all sorts of legalism.

With Ockham we are confronted with what can be called an "extrinsicist" concept of action: not in himself or in the goodness of the object does man find sufficient reasons for choosing one act or another; he chooses under the influence of an element outside himself, hence, the name extrinsicism. Once again we perceive the radical change of concept in this way of thinking about the good and this way of tending toward it.

If there is no longer an attraction that impels us toward the good, that means that man no longer has within himself what Saint Thomas called the "natural inclinations", which he made a key feature of his moral doctrine.[15] Natural inclinations are "natural" dispositions, which is to say that they are dependent on the spiritual nature of man, potentialities of the whole person that set him in motion toward his own activity. They are the basis of the natural law.[16] By virtue of being created in the image and likeness

[15] Cf. *Summa Theologiae* I-II, q. 94, a. 3 and 4, corpus.

[16] According to the *Catechism of the Catholic Church* [hereafter abbreviated CCC], "The 'divine and natural' law shows man the way to follow so as to

of God, man is naturally oriented toward the truth, toward the good, toward God, toward the opposite sex, toward the preservation of life. Founded on these inclinations, freedom is qualified by the attraction that it spontaneously experiences to what is true and good, or at least to what appears to it as such. Thus man is free, not *despite* his natural inclinations, but on the contrary *because* of them. Of course man can be mistaken, but even sin does not present an obstacle to these natural inclinations. If man chooses evil, it is not because he was attracted by evil, as we have already explained earlier, but rather because evil, in the particular situation in which he finds himself, appears to him as a good—a deceptive one, no doubt, but as a good.

Ockham, in contrast, considers these natural inclinations to be blind tendencies in which reason, contrary to what we find in the writings of Saint Thomas, does not intervene at all. Saint Thomas spoke about an "instinct of reason" (*instinctus rationis* or *rationalis*): the natural inclinations enable us to acquire an instinct that is permeated by reason. Ockham, though, rejects the natural inclinations because they seem to him to impair freedom: if man is naturally oriented toward the good, Ockham thinks, then he is no longer free!

Having rejected the natural inclinations, Ockham also rejects the *habitus*, which he now understands as mere habits.

---

practice the good and attain his end. The natural law states the first and essential precepts which govern the moral life. It hinges upon the desire for God and submission to him, who is the source and judge of all that is good, as well as upon the sense that the other is one's equal. Its principal precepts are expressed in the Decalogue. This law is called 'natural,' not in reference to the nature of irrational beings, but because reason which decrees it properly belongs to human nature" (CCC 1955).

We can repeat here the example of the violinist that was mentioned earlier: Is the possibility of playing wrong notes what makes the violinist free? Or, from another perspective: Does the fact that he no longer plays wrong notes really impair his freedom? Or, on the contrary, is it not the pinnacle of freedom to be capable of no longer playing wrong notes?

Finally, as the ultimate consequence of this new concept of freedom, action loses its unity. We can speak about an "atomization" of action. The overall finality or purpose is lost. There is only a proximate, short-term finality. Every act is altogether separate from those that precede it and from those that follow it. Every act, like an atom, becomes an isolated case, independent from the rest of activity. This would give rise to a new discipline of moral theology, "casuistry", which considered acts exclusively as "cases of conscience".

If, according to William of Ockham, natural inclinations are a blow to man's freedom, if the same goes for the virtues or the *habitus*, if every act is a little entity in itself, independent from the finality of the action, how will man be able to choose? An external, extrinsic element is necessary, we said. This element is the law. But what law? Ockham replies: God's law. In fact, confronting human freedom there is another freedom, divine freedom, which is the epitome of indifference. Ockham pushes his argument still farther. God decreed the commandments in the Decalogue "by indifference". He could have decreed something else. He could have said: "Thou shalt kill", "Thou shalt commit adultery", and then that is what it would have been necessary to do! This gives rise to the morality of obligation, legalism. Since the goodness of my activity is no longer within that activity, an additional external element is needed to impel me to choose. This element is God's law. Man acts in terms of a law that is no longer inscribed within him but is totally external and foreign to him, a law that is totally arbitrary, which man can carry out only by God's decree.

Is there anything wrong with this reasoning? At first nothing changes concretely. We do continue to follow God's law, manifested by the commandments of the Decalogue. What changes, however, is the *reason* why we do this. We no longer obey the Decalogue because there is some goodness intrinsic to the commandment. We obey the Decalogue simply because God commands it, independently of any value that is good in itself. As you can guess, once God's authority is called into question, everything will collapse. People will go so far as to ask: "Who is God to impose that on me?" In rejecting God's authority, they will end up rejecting the cogency of the divine law and, finally, they will call into question the goodness and relevance of God's commandments. They will then turn to the law of men or, more precisely, to the law of the strongest.

This is the rise of *authoritarianism*. From now on every authority will be tempted to think that whatever it requires is good, by reason of the very fact that it requires it. The authority will then have great difficulty in calling itself into question. The risk of a sectarian or dictatorial trend is significant. If the law of the strongest is the criterion for the good, dictatorship is practically inevitable, and any questioning of the law in terms of a superior Law is considered by the authority to be a threat or even a crime. Recent totalitarian governments, unfortunately, have illustrated this development perfectly.

Kantian morality[17] would take Ockham's point of view even farther: the goodness of an act comes solely from its obligatory character, so much so that if man ever derives a bit of pleasure from what he does, the act is no longer moral. The more obligatory it is, the more contrary to man's profound aspirations, the better it is! Jansenism would very easily be engulfed in this sort of thinking. Still later, when God's authority would no longer be acknowledged, some would try to reach an agreement on several common points: this would be called consensual morality. The current debate on questions of bioethics clearly reflects this problematic approach: what is "permitted" by the law becomes "good" at the moral level. Take the tragic example of abortion: it is denounced as a crime in Scripture, is condemned by the Hippocratic Oath,[18] and has always been considered by the Church to be a very seriously immoral act that is never justifiable. When a country votes for a law authorizing abortion, can it thereby change the moral value of that act? Certainly not! And yet, unfortunately, legal authorization insidiously brings with it the idea that it is not an evil, since the law permits it. We can easily see the tragic consequences of this legalistic concept of morality.

[17] Immanuel Kant, German idealist philosopher (1724–1804).
[18] Oath composed in the fourth century B.C., traditionally taken by physicians in the West before they begin to practice medicine.

We are confronted with two models of moral theology. We can call them: "third-person morality" and "first-person morality".[19]

Third-person morality is the morality of the external observer, who considers the act from outside, as something isolated, and sees the goodness or malice of the act in terms of the law, in terms of whether or not it conforms to the law. In third-person morality, the two prevalent elements are the *law* and *conscience*, conscience here being understood as what allows me, in certain cases, to elude the law. In this concept, the law is general. It must then be "applied", mathematically, as it were, to particular cases. However, since the law can never foresee all possible cases, there are cases to which the law does not apply. In these cases, man uses an instrument, his conscience, which allows him to liberate himself from the law.

The morality of Saint Thomas, in contrast, is a *first-person* morality: what matters is the *subject* who develops himself in his activity. The reader would search in vain for a treatise on conscience in the second part of the *Summa Theologiae*. Saint Thomas speaks only about "synderesis", which is the highest part of the conscience, the voice that man hears saying to him, in the depths of his being, "Do good and avoid evil."[20] The encyclical *Veritatis splendor* by John Paul II forcefully reiterates this first-person approach: in order to evaluate the morality of an act truly, it is ab-

[19] Servais Pinckaers, *Morality: The Catholic View*, trans. Michael Sherwin (South Bend, Ind.: St. Augustine's Press, 2001), 32–41.

[20] We see here the connection between synderesis and the natural law, that light of the intellect placed within us by God, by which we know what must be done and what must be avoided.

solutely necessary to put oneself in the perspective of the acting person.[21] To put it differently, the person participates in constructing his activity. The cardinal virtue of prudence intervenes here as a virtue of practical reason that enables me, in whatever circumstances I may find myself, not to apply a general law to my particular case, but rather to construct my activity in an altogether new way that was never preestablished but is truly personal and singular. This is precisely the way in which the saints act. The saints manifest an extraordinary originality and inventiveness. The saints are not content to apply a law. In a way that is ever new, they construct their own activity under the movement of the Holy Spirit.

The new concept of freedom—and the new concept of moral theology that results from it—has still further consequences, notably the separation of the different areas of theology.

First of all, the separation of morality from Scripture. Since the only thing of interest to morality is to know what I should do, people will take an interest only in the normative passages of Scripture, so as not to fall into sin. Therefore they keep the Decalogue and several exhortations by Saint Paul, but they abandon the Sermon on the Mount, which was, however, in the opinion of Saint Augustine, the *Magna Carta*, the great charter of the moral life. They also abandon all the wisdom literature. The only parts of Scripture that are kept are those that are immediately normative for human action.

---

[21] Cf. John Paul II, encyclical *Veritatis splendor* (August 6, 1993), no. 78.

Then there is a division between dogmatic and moral theology. On the one hand, we have *dogmatic* theology, in other words, "what must be believed"; on the other hand, we have *moral* theology, in other words, "what must be done so as not to sin". A third area appears, *pastoral* theology, which concerns preaching and administering the sacraments. This area is totally disconnected from what must be believed and what must be done.

Finally, there is a tragic separation between moral and spiritual theology. *Moral* theology is what belongs to the realm of obligatory things. *Spirituality* is something "beyond" the law, reserved for an elite. Morality now concerns only the minimum requirements, beneath which I sin. Consequently, the beatitudes and the gifts of the Holy Spirit disappear from all the manuals of moral theology. As for spiritual theology, it is subdivided into *ascetical* and *mystical* theology. Ascetical theology includes everything that one must do voluntarily. This concerns religious, who are the only ones called to perfection. As for mystical theology, it concerns extraordinary states such as ecstasies or levitations. In a word, morality becomes activity without the spirit, and spirituality becomes spirit without activity.

This separation of the different areas of theology may offer practical advantages in the establishment of programs of study; nonetheless, it is extremely harmful to the unity of theology. In making divisions between different theological disciplines, there is always the risk of losing sight of the unity of God's loving plan in Jesus Christ. In the case of our subject, acedia, these divisions and separations would not be inconsequential.

In this context, what actually became of acedia? It is easy to understand that it no longer had much of a place in moral theology. Starting with the first great commentators on Saint Thomas, Cajetan (1469–1534), Suarez (1548–1617), and John of Saint Thomas (1589–1644), acedia is no longer situated at all within the context of action. In all the manuals of moral theology that followed, until the Second Vatican Council, you will search in vain for any discussion of acedia. It reappears, albeit transformed, in works of spirituality. This occurs then along two lines:

—it appears as a kind of *sloth*, lukewarmness, negligence in prayer, but not in the pregnant sense of neglecting observances, as in the writings of Evagrius. It is simply on the order of distraction.

—It also appears in a completely different sort of literature, in the form of *melancholy*, as is the case in the writings of Petrarch (1304–1374) or Baudelaire (1821–1867). The reader will find then praises of tedium or of *spleen*. This illustrates a certain complacency in a kind of ill-being.

If you take the two definitions of acedia that we mentioned in the writings of Saint Thomas Aquinas, the "sadness about spiritual good" and "disgust with action", and you abandon the unified concept of Christian action in which the Holy Spirit and Christ are at the very heart of this action, you will see that the sadness becomes "melancholy" and the paralysis of action becomes "sloth" . . .

However, although the notion of acedia has disappeared from theological and spiritual reflection, has it really disappeared from our lives? This is what we still have to examine now.

3

The Relevance of Acedia
in Christian Life

In the preceding pages we made a long historical survey that enabled us to discover the seriousness and complexity of acedia. Our rather detailed study of Evagrius and Saint Thomas Aquinas, in particular, led us to perceive the terrible character of an evil that causes man to lose the joy of living and paralyzes his interior dynamism. We have seen, too, that, starting with the modern era, the very term "acedia" has gradually disappeared from the vocabulary of experience, only to be replaced by words that, although they do express something about acedia, nevertheless do not give a clear idea of all the connotations that the *akèdia* of the first monks included within it.

Gloominess, weariness, dejection, sadness, discouragement, disgust with everything, melancholy, boredom, sloth, mediocrity, being "down" . . . All these things are behind our *acedia*, even though, once again, acedia cannot be reduced to any one of these concepts. Now who among us can say that he has not encountered one of these ills, near or far, firsthand or among his acquaintances? Whether individually or collectively, morale is rarely a long-lasting fair weather system. My purpose is not to analyze the causes of the rather disillusioned outlook of our modern world.

After the preceding historical survey, I simply wish to suggest a few lines of thought about the current relevance of acedia *in the life of a Christian*, in other words, in the life of someone who, by his baptismal vocation, is already a member of the Body of Christ and is tending toward full participation in the life of God, sometimes even without being very much aware of it.

The Disintegration of the Human Person

Let us begin with what is no doubt the most radical and most tragic manifestation: acedia can appear as a veritable disintegration of the human person.

The loss of meaning

Someone remarked that "the moral life is the choice to make sense out of the time that passes."[1] This is quite true if we retain both connotations of the word "sense": *meaning* and *orientation*. Remember that Saint Thomas presented moral action as being directed toward a goal: the vision of God, in other words, participation in his own life. This goal is what gives action its meaning, its sense, so that this action can become an anticipation of beatitude and a preparation for it. From this perspective, acedia appears as the temptation to make *nonsense* out of the moral life. Thus the profoundly immoral character of this vice becomes evident: acedia admits that absurdity might be the

[1] X. Thévenot, *Avance en eau profonde! Carnet spirituel* (Paris: Cerf and DDB, 1997), 45.

last word in human life. Can we not compare it, then, to what Sartre called "nausea"?

> The word absurdity is coming to life under my pen; a little while ago, in the garden, I couldn't find it, but neither was I looking for it, I didn't need it: I thought without words, *on* things, *with* things. Absurdity was not an idea in my head, or the sound of a voice, only this long serpent dead at my feet, this wooden serpent. Serpent or claw or root or vulture's talon, what difference does it make. And without formulating anything clearly, I understood that I had found the key to Existence, the key to my Nauseas, to my own life. In fact, all that I could grasp beyond that returns to this fundamental absurdity.[2]

No doubt we are confronted here with the most dangerous aspect of acedia: the temptation of *nihilism*. This is a genuine hatred of being, a dislocation of the human person from the universe of being, in other words, an uprooting of man from his proper place: in a word, it is man's departure from his dwelling. We can see in this also one of the most serious perils for the dignity of the human person: a veritable spiritual depression. Indeed, nihilism deems reality to be unintelligible, devoid of sense in itself and for itself: the very concept of truth is rejected as non-sense. Nihilism denies that there is a dynamic of human life:

> Here gloominess finally removes its mask: its true name is nihilism, the loss of the joy of being that is offered and waits under the fragile appearances of a temporal order with sense, that is to say, one that is oriented and meaningful. For nihilism, the past is dead, and the future leads to death. What good does it do to remember and to become

[2] Jean-Paul Sartre, *Nausea*, trans. Lloyd Alexander (New York: New Directions, 1964), 173.

involved, what good does it do to hope? When the meaning of time is lost in this way, through a mixture of boredom and satiety, the very sense of being is modified.[3]

We see here the impressive perspicacity of the Thomistic insight into the danger to action posed by acedia: acedia, in Thomas' view, prevented any orientation toward the final end; nihilism confirms this and even goes a step farther: it purely and simply denies the possibility of an end. Acedia then manifests the will to be rid of God; man wanted to advance his self-creation, but it only led to non-sense:

> Everything is happening as though we broke the implicit contract with God around two centuries ago and accepted the devil's bargain. . . . Satan offered us power, the knowledge of good and evil, eternal happiness, on the condition that we renounce God. We renounced God, and the devil granted our wish. . . . But we are approaching the end of the agreement, and we are coming to understand that it was a fool's contract. We possess everything, but we do not have God. We have power, but we have lost meaning. Our society [which] is oozing with anxiety . . . is going to disappear.[4]

The temptation of despair

When the meaning of life disappears, acedia then engenders its first daughter, the most terrible of all: despair! Such a lack of hope is, alas, quite common among our contemporaries and, even more seriously, among young people. Are we not experiencing here the ultimate consequences of the new concept of freedom introduced by Ockham? Freedom—understood no longer as the acceptance of our

[3] M. Léna, "Éloge du temps ordinaire", *Christus* 157 (1993): 22.

[4] X. Emmanuelli, in *Famille Chrétienne* (March 12, 1998).

orientation to the good, but as the possibility of doing what we want—has claimed to be without limits. But instead of bringing about happiness, it has, on the contrary, only made the feeling of dissatisfaction crueler. We find this expressed admirably by Joseph Ratzinger:

> Today, when the promises of unlimited freedom have been made the most of, we are beginning to understand afresh this saying about the "sorrow of the world." The forbidden joys lose their attraction the moment they are no longer forbidden. They had and have to be radicalized, the pitch increasingly raised, and nevertheless seem finally flat and stale because they are all finite while the hunger is for the infinite.[5]

The fall of the idols that man had set up for himself in place of God now causes him to sink into despair:

> Everywhere we are seeing the fall of the idols—science, progress—which have lost their prestige. They have become what they should never have ceased to be: tools in the hands of man with which one can build good things and bad, temples and tombs. All this has led in broad sectors to a feeling of "disenchantment" and disillusionment, boredom, sadness, solitude, depression, among all those who do not find a renewed sense of life. Our age is marked by a great spiritual "void"; *taedium vitae* and *acedia* are found again in many of our contemporaries.[6]

Now Saint Thomas showed clearly that the root of despair is to be sought in acedia. Acedia is a lack of love, the lack of the great Love; it shatters the impulse of hope and

---

[5] Joseph Ratzinger, *To Look on Christ: Exercises in Faith, Hope and Love*, trans. Robert Nowell (New York: Crossroad, 1991), 69.

[6] Cf. G. Danneels, "Intervention au VIe Symposium des Evêques d'Europe, à Rome, en octobre 1985", DC 1906 (1985): 1073.

threatens to lead to the rejection of life itself. It is a real *flirtation with death*, according to the words of the future Benedict XVI:

> The deepest root of this sorrow is the lack of any great hope and the unattainability of any great love: everything one can hope for is known, and all love becomes the disappointment of finiteness in a world whose monstrous surrogates are only a pitiful disguise for profound despair. And in this way the truth becomes ever more tangible that the sorrow of the world leads to death: it is only flirting with death, the ghastly business of playing with power and violence, that is still exciting enough to create an appearance of satisfaction. "If you eat it, you must die"—for a long time this has no longer been just a saying from mythology (Gen 3:17).[7]

Acedia is at the source of the despair of our contemporaries, who think that it would be better not to exist: it is truly that sin against the Holy Spirit which refuses to receive Love and forgiveness. Joseph Ratzinger again says it forcefully:

> In the Christian system of virtues, despair, that is to say, the radical antithesis of faith and hope, is labelled as the sin against the Holy Spirit because it excludes the latter's power to heal and to forgive and thereby rejects salvation. Corresponding to this is the fact that in the new religion "pessimism" is the sin of all sins, for to doubt optimism, progress, utopia is a frontal attack on the spirit of the modern age: it is to dispute its fundamental creed on which its security rests, even though this is always under threat in view of the weakness of the sham god of history.[8]

---

[7] Ratzinger, *To Look on Christ*, 69–70.
[8] Cf. ibid., 43. See also John Paul II, encyclical *Dominum et vivificantem*, no.

Evagrius was not wrong when he said that acedia threatened to hurl man into the yawning chasm of self-destruction:

We had to shake off the Big Brother God who is spying on us in order to be free, take back into ourselves the God projected into the heavens and ourselves rule over creation as God. Thus there arose in fact a kind of spirit and will that was and is opposed to life and is a dominion of death. The more perceptible this becomes the more the original intention turns into its opposite while remaining trapped in the same point of departure: man who only wanted to be his own creator and to reassemble creation himself with a better form of evolution he had thought out himself—this man ends in self-negation and self-destruction. He finds it would be better if he were not there.[9]

Instability: The Spatial Dimension

Let us move on to the second manifestation of acedia: instability. When we presented Evagrius' teaching about acedia, I emphasized that it involved two essential components: a spatial dimension (the cell) and a temporal dimension (the sixth hour). Let us begin by returning to the spatial dimension; then we will look at the temporal dimension.

It is a cliché to say that our contemporaries are unstable. It is however, alas, a statement that is well founded in reality. You will remember that among the anchorites

46: "The blasphemy against the Holy Spirit consists precisely in the radical refusal to accept this forgiveness."

[9] Ratzinger, To Look on Christ, 70–71.

of the desert, the desire to leave their cell was the most significant manifestation of acedia. Any pretext would do to leave their dwelling and the stifling impression that it made. Let us listen, for example, to this short passage by John Cassian:

> [The monk afflicted with acedia] says that everything about him is rough, and not only that there is nothing edifying among the brethren who are staying there, but also that even food for the body cannot be procured without great difficulty. Lastly he fancies that he will never be well while he stays in that place, unless he leaves his cell (in which he is sure to die if he stays in it any longer).[10]

Now let us not imagine that the trials of the fifth-century hermits died with them! No doubt, the instability from which our contemporaries suffer is not that far removed from the sort that tempted the cenobites in the desert . . .

The perpetual need for change

This instability is manifested first of all by a constant need to move, to change. To change one's locality, work, situation, institution, occupation, spouse, friends . . . A twelfth-century author, Galand de Reigny, personified acedia and made her speak, in a very humorous dialogue, with the other vices. Here are the words that he puts in her mouth:

> I seek to kill time by chattering, it matters little about what. For if I do not spend the day babbling or going for a stroll, I die of boredom. . . . Roaming around or rambling on— that is what gives me strength! Listening to gossips, seeing new things, what bliss, in my view! I wish that every

[10] John Cassian, *The Institutes* X, 2, NPNF-2 11:267a, slightly modernized.

day there would be a change in government, new legisla-
tion, modifications in institutions, so as to obtain, thanks
to these changes, some remedy for my boredom. For everything that lasts horrifies me; I abhor seeing something remain in the same state.[11]

We are witnessing, therefore, a frenzy of novelty and,
ipso facto, a horror of anything lasting, of everything that
stays in one place. Both are the sign of general dissatisfaction: as soon as someone has obtained what he desires, he
wants something else, just as children do. Someone begins
reading a book but does not finish it; someone else enrolls
in a course but stops going to class, and so on. Could we
not, following Father de Finance, describe this constant
search for change as a "passing through"? In terms of desire, Finance in fact distinguishes between *passing through*
[*passage*] and *passing beyond* [*dépassement*]. Passing through
is a continual gliding from one thing to another, on the
horizontal level,[12] which can degenerate into a craze for
traveling or instability.[13] Passing beyond, in contrast, is a
vertical movement that draws one toward a higher order of
values and, finally, to God. One could say then that acedia
is the temptation to reject *passing beyond* and to stick with
passing through, thus losing sight of the dynamic of desire,
which is the dynamic of love.[14]

[11] Galand de Reigny, *Parabolaire* 16, 7 (SC 378) (Paris: Cerf, 1992), 279–
81.

[12] See J. de Finance, *Essai sur l'agir human*, 2nd ed. (Brussels: Culture et
Vérité, 1997), 105.

[13] Ibid., 106: "This perpetual dissatisfaction can degenerate into instability,
into a craze for traveling, or it may also become aggravated as pessimism and
resentment."

[14] Father de Finance in fact considers various sorts of *passing beyond*, the last

Might not the culture of "channel-surfing" be one sign of this acedia? Besides a simple desire to see everything at once, hopping from one program to another is the manifestation of a radical instability of the human being, who is always tempted by easy access (*passing through*) to goods that are immediately available, instead of the costly but constructive effort of *passing beyond*, with a view to attaining a goal, an end. Acedia results in the disappearance of major life projects and commitments that require self-giving and even self-sacrifice:

> To facilitate repeated adaptations to an ever-changing present, narcissistic apathy, an unstable self, is better suited, since it alone is capable of evolving in a simultaneous movement: "The end of the will coincides with the era of pure indifference, with the disappearance of the major goals and great enterprises for which life deserves to be sacrificed."[15]

Flight from self and flight from God

Evagrius had already shrewdly pointed out that the desire to leave one's cell is, in reality, a flight: the flight from oneself. The spatial dimension broadens, or, rather, becomes deeper and interior: it concerns no longer just the cell but the individual himself. He no longer knows how to be alone. Furthermore, he is afraid of being alone. For in solitude one discovers what one is like, with no cosmetics

---

of which, called "absolute transcendence", brings man toward the Absolute, toward God. Desire transcends itself then in love, or, better yet, "the love is already there, at the root of desire" (168). We see here the comparison that can be made with the Thomistic doctrine of the circularity of love and of acedia as love growing cold.

[15] Cf. C. Flipo, "L'acédie dans la tradition spirituelle", *Christus* 157 (1993): 60.

or mask; one is forced to confront one's misery, spiritual and moral poverty. I do not play a role for long when I am alone, since there is no one to observe me except myself . . . Then I see myself as I am, and this spectacle is unbearable! Acedia is thus a flight from self.

But is it not also a flight from God? Indeed, sometimes we get the impression that acedia is instead a search for oneself and a flight from God. Ratzinger again puts it well:

> [The] nature [of acedia] is the flight from God, the wish to be alone with oneself and one's finiteness and not to be disturbed by the presence of God.[16]

Had Israel not already found it too demanding to be God's chosen people? It would have preferred to return to Egypt (cf. Num 14:2–4), in other words, to return to normalcy, to stop being God's elect. Now Israel's ordeal can be considered the paradigm of any test of freedom. The temptation that the chosen people experienced is ultimately, for every human being, an image of the temptation to reject his own greatness.

The rejection of one's own greatness

Remember that one of the daughters of acedia, according to Saint Thomas, is *faint-heartedness*. "Pusillanimity" (the Latinate term for it) is the vice opposed to the virtue called *magnanimity*, greatness of soul. It is the inability to believe in the greatness of the vocation to which God is calling us: to become sharers in the divine nature. The future Benedict XVI comments that modern man does not have the courage to attain his full grandeur:

[16] Ratzinger, *To Look on Christ*, 71.

[He] wants to be "more realistic." Metaphysical inertia would on this account be identical with that false humility that has become so common today: man does not want to believe that God is concerned about him, knows him, loves him, watches over him, is close to him.[17]

Ultimately we find again the genuine hatred of being about which we spoke earlier, the hatred that drives man to accept his own destruction:

The first source of acedia is a lack of magnanimity—a quite forgotten virtue that is based on the correct view of the dignity of our human vocation: the man who claims to be a "realist" refuses to believe that he is destined to live in God and with God. Thus despair arises from a hatred of man, and this hatred often assumes the form of a supposedly scientific reduction of his humanity to the animal state: man is an ape that walks upright. In deep ecology (cf. Eugen Drewermann), this hatred is even more radical and becomes an attitude of self-punishment whereby man, guilty of tyranny with regard to nature, repairs the wrong committed against it by accepting his own destruction.[18]

Incidentally, it is astonishing to see how, in the beginning, man was tempted by pride: he wanted "to be like God" (Gen 3:5); in other words, he wanted to become God without God or against God. That was *presumption*. Today we are witnessing the opposite temptation: people think it would be better not to exist; this is faint-heartedness.

Today there is a remarkable hatred among people for their own real greatness. Man sees himself as the enemy of life,

---

[17] Ibid., 70.

[18] P. Ide, "Soyez toujours prêts à rendre compte de la désespérance qui est en vous!" *Sources Vives* 80 (1998): 14.

of the balance of creation, as the great disturber of the peace of nature (which would be better off if he did not exist), as the creature that went wrong. His salvation and the salvation of the world would on this view consist of his disappearing, of his life and soul being taken back from him, of what is specifically human vanishing so that nature could return to its unconscious perfection in its own rhythm and with its own wisdom of dying and coming into being.[19]

Now presumption and pusillanimity are precisely the two vices that Saint Thomas opposes to magnanimity, one by excess, the other by defect.

The soul has given itself to God, but then finds that fidelity to this donation is an insurmountable ordeal. Given this failure of the will, man must again be reminded of his own greatness, as Pope Saint Leo preached forcefully in the fifth century[20] and as Josef Pieper prophesied in 1935.[21] It is necessary to rediscover the Thomistic intuition about the role of Christ's Incarnation, which we saw earlier: Christ came to restore to us the hope of arriving at our vocation as sons and daughters in the Son; he came to remind us of our own greatness and to reopen for us the way to heaven. Furthermore, by his Resurrection, he himself takes us on his shoulders to carry us to the Father.

We might add that the greatness of the human vocation is not limited to the individual aspect of human life; it

[19] Ratzinger, To Look on Christ, 70.

[20] Leo the Great, Sermo 21 in nat. Dom., 3 (PL 54:192C, cited in the CCC 1691): "Christian, recognize your dignity."

[21] Josef Pieper, Lieben—hoffen—glauben (Munich, 1986), 232: "It is not through 'working' that one annihilates despair (at least consciousness of it) but only through the clear-sighted greatness of spirit that the greatness of one's own existence expects and demands and through the blessed encouragement of hope in eternal life" (quoted in Ratzinger, To Look on Christ, 72).

must extend to all of society so that it may be truly free and human:

> A society that turns what is specifically human into something purely private . . . will of its nature be sorrowful, a place of despair: it rests on a diminution of human dignity. A society whose public order is consistently determined by agnosticism is not a society that has become free but a society that has despaired, marked by the sorrow of man who is fleeing God and in contradiction with himself.[22]

Thus we can say that our era is characterized by a certain "cultural acedia". Given this situation, Christians have the responsibility to know how to give an account of their faith: it is in this way that they will contribute to the battle against the fragmentation of knowledge that this acedia manifests.

False humility or sadness over good

The rejection of man's greatness and of the vocation to which he is called may be hidden subtly behind a semblance of humility: man asserts that he is not worthy of God's love. But such a reaction manifests, once again, a perspective that is excessively man-centered; in reality, God is the one who loved us first (1 Jn 4:10), without any merit on our part (Rom 5:8). God's love does not depend on our personal sanctity; rather, our sanctity depends on God's love for us and should be our free and loving response to it. This is why the semblance of modesty is, in reality, the worst form of pride, which refuses to accept the infinite so as to be content with what is within its reach. This is the temptation to be "reasonable":

---

[22] Ratzinger, *To Look on Christ*, 72.

Deep inside us there is a sly resistance. I think that the deepest and most irremediable pride—that of the angels, perhaps—consists of refusing to accept the infinite so as to "be content" with what is within our reach. Such pride decks itself out in the appearances of humility: "I do not ask for that much, I do not aim so high! This infinite happiness is very beautiful, but it is too much for me." And secretly we think: "That is beyond me because it does not come from me." . . . Satan often inspires in us this attitude of modesty, which is the worst form of self-sufficiency and the refusal to go beyond one's depth. We just hope that we will not be devoured either by Good or by Evil. Satan urges us to be a reasonable man, who is drawn by nothing—neither by the folly of darkness nor by the folly of Love. The virtuous man must be nobody's fool, not even of joy . . . not even of God. This is the sin to which the curse in the Book of Revelation applies: "If you were hot or cold. . . ." It is better to take the wrong infinity than to renounce the infinite![23]

Saint Thomas, moreover, in the response to one of the objections that he proposed, very subtly analyzed the error of identifying acedia with humility.[24] Humility, indeed, is not self-deprecation; it is good, on the contrary, always to aim higher, as long as we do not rely on our own strength but place our trust in God's help. Recall too how, in the *Summa contra Gentiles*, he denounced the subtle temptation to lower the object of one's desire and to be content with a "bestial happiness".

This rejection of man's greatness can also be manifested, more subtly, by sadness over the good that one sees others

[23] M.-D. Molinié, "Du désespoir à l'adoration", *Famille Chrétienne* 1161 (April 13, 2000): 9–10.
[24] *Summa Theologiae*, II-II, q. 35, a. 1, ad 3.

do. Saint Thomas explained that acedia was a pernicious sadness because it is a response to good and not to evil. Now it may happen that one becomes sad, not over a brother's fault, but on the contrary over his virtues, because they show us our own negligence; the faults of our brethren, on the contrary, often elicit a secret complaisance, for they seem to legitimize our own defects. Still others may be prompted to denounce in other people defects similar to their own, because a human being always has difficulty accepting the humiliation of seeing the defective image of himself reflected in another.

Duration: The Temporal Dimension

After the spatial dimension, let us now consider the temporal dimension. This, too, has some surprises for us with its relevance. Whereas an angel acts by means of a single act, man needs multiple acts, because he is subject to time. Now the danger of acedia lies precisely in the fact that it utilizes this essential dimension of the human being: his being situated in time, in an era, in a precise moment of history. With the passage of time, one loses interest and incentive. The day comes when one no longer enjoys anything. Everything bores us and burdens us. What used to motivate us spiritually has lost all its attraction, and the mainspring of our activity seems to be broken. Here again, the people of Israel have been there: after a certain time they were disgusted with the manna (cf. Num 21:5), which, however, was a miraculous food given by God and adapted to each one's taste (cf. Wis 16:20–21). Moreover, Saint Thomas cited this experience of Israel in making the point that acedia was "a certain disgust of working" ("quoddam taedium operandi", *S.Th.* II-II, q. 35, a. 1). Let us therefore review here the manifestations of acedia connected, in some way, with time.

The noonday devil

We have seen how tradition, following Evagrius, identified acedia with the noonday devil of Psalm 90:6 [Douay-Rheims; cf. Ps 91:6 RSVC]. Now if we reflect carefully, we must acknowledge that the devil is usually associated with night, not with broad daylight. Hence the terrible character of the noonday devil! Evagrius had already pointed out how this devil made sure that the person with acedia did not realize his condition. The very disappearance of the word serves the devil's purpose: How can one fear an evil when one does not even know its name? Therefore, who would fear the devil in broad daylight? It is precisely at noon, however, that the "most oppressive" of all the demons attacks, as Evagrius says.

Acedia is formidable above all when the tropical sun seems as though it will never descend from its zenith, where it appears to be fixed forever and ever. The zenith is precisely the moment when there is no shadow. In the morning or the evening, we see the shadows move, and we are well aware of the passage of time. At the zenith, in contrast, there is no shadow; in other words, there is no "mystery". The human, philosophical, and even theological sciences must be capable of "explaining" everything. We saw earlier that acedia would engender despair, the first sin against hope; but there is also a camouflaged form of despair: ideological optimism. The latter is based on a boundless confidence in the progress of humanity and science. Therefore it is necessary to accept nothing that cannot be verified, demonstrated, or experienced by reason.

> How many times have we heard this sentence, which is typical of ideological optimism: "Today, science does not know, but someday it will know; today technology cannot do it, but it has already made such advances that nobody can deny that it will be able to do it someday." The latest utopia is that of perfect health. How many patients think that this has become not only a possibility but a right?[25]

This was precisely the point of departure for the Cartesian method: the first precept of science was not to accept anything as true unless one knew from evidence that it was. Faith is thus excluded, on methodical principle; from then on, the chasm between science and faith got deeper and deeper.

However, while we are traveling, the areas of shadow blend with the areas of brightness, and it is better that way: too much light, indeed, hurts the eyes . . . If we are capable of listening to the voice of Christ that guides the Church and resonates within her, we will need less light on our journey. When someone is holding our hand, we can advance easily in the darkness. Now Christ, the Light of the world, holds our hand to guide us, through the night of faith, to the Father (Jn 14:6), and he gives us his Spirit to lead us into the fullness of truth (Jn 16:13).

There is no longer any reason, then, to fear the darkness, since the Lord guides us by his Word. It is enough to be willing to receive the message of truth, which is freedom

---

[25] Ide, "Soyez toujours prêts", 14.

and communion. Thus the true light will be able to shine, the one that allows us to utilize all our faculties of intellect and heart—in other words, Christ himself: "I have come as light into the world, that whoever believes in me may not remain in darkness" (Jn 12:46). Ideological optimism is an ersatz hope; true hope surprises, surpasses immediate expectations and possibilities: it is the promise of a gift beyond our capacities.

Noon is not only the hour when there is no shadow. It is also the moment when the sun seems to have halted and when time, which it measures, also appears to stop and hang heavy. That is when the present instant threatens to become unbearable. Two reactions are possible then: losing the sense of time, both past and future, as nihilism does;[26] or else, on the contrary, fleeing the present and taking refuge in the past or in the future.

As a reaction to the gloominess of the present there may indeed be a tendency to cultivate an excessive nostalgia for the successful, well-spent moments of the past. To embellish it, to delight in it, to tell stories about it. When nothing goes well any more in the present, it is so reassuring to become attached to the past, when one "did so many good things". Then, one tells stories . . . to oneself or to others. Or else one plunges ahead into the future, since that is the plaything of the imagination and of dreams. Often, however, the flight into the past or the escape into the future produces nothing but sadness and disgust; one finds in them a taste of bitterness and dissatisfaction:

---

[26] See M. Léna, "Éloge du temps ordinaire", 22: "In the case of nihilism, the past is dead, and the future leads to death."

> We must not imagine that Sisyphus was happy while he was rolling his rock: the horrible symmetry of yesterday and tomorrow could only foster in him a gloomy mood. He transports a stone that will never be a cathedral.[27]

Usually, when confronting the suspension of time and the void of boredom, the most classic strategy is to try to "kill time", as we say. No doubt it is not insignificant that this idiomatic expression uses the verb "to kill", which relates boredom to *hatred*. Now time is not killed; on the contrary, it is necessary to *wed* it, in other words, to cling to the present moment and to live it in all its spiritual intensity. Since acedia creates an empty space, people try to "furnish" it: this is Pascal's famous diversion or *amusement*:

> I have discovered that all human misfortune comes from one thing, which is not knowing how to remain quietly in one room. A man who has sufficient means to live, if he knew how to stay at home happily, would not go forth to go on the sea or to a siege. No one would buy a commission in the army so dearly were it not intolerable not to stir out of the town, and no one would seek conversation and the amusement of games but that no one can with pleasure remain in his own house.[28]

We can also note the close connection between the persistence of time and, on the contrary, the flight of charity in others.[29] Indeed, the Greek word used by Evagrius to indicate this disappearance of charity (*écleipein*) literally

---

[27] Ibid., 22–23.

[28] Blaise Pascal, *Pensées*, no. 139, in *Pensées and the Provincial Letters*, Modern Library Books (New York: Random House, 1941), p. 48.

[29] Evagrius, *Praktikos*, or *The Monk: A Treatise on the Practical Life*, in *Evagrius of Pontus: The Greek Ascetic Corpus*, trans. with introduction and commentary by Robert E. Sinkewicz, Oxford Early Christian Studies (Oxford and New

means *to eclipse*, and this is certainly not used accidentally.[30] The oppressive light of the sun and the night of charity are two aspects of the same phenomenon, so that one can be the suitable metaphor for the other; because love of neighbor supposes a relation to time that is rendered impossible here. If only the present exists, one cannot love:

> We can love only what is absent and, in order to love what is present, we must imagine its absence (cf. Plato, *Symposium*, 200, a–e). Love can persist only if it hollows out an additional dimension in the present, the possibility of its absence. Its joy is to see the presence triumph incessantly there over the absence.[31]

The temptation of doubt

When everything is dark, when time weighs heavily, doubt appears: you see neither the destination nor even the way leading to it on which you thought you were walking. Then you say to yourself: "What if all this was just an illusion? What if the material world was the only reality after all? What if there was nothing beyond what I can see, hear, and touch?" A terrible temptation that was not spared the saints, as this short passage by Saint Thérèse of the Child Jesus shows:

York: Oxford Univ. Press, 2003), 99. 12: "And further, he instils in him . . . the idea that love has disappeared from among the brothers and there is no one to console him."

[30] As was very astutely remarked by Rémi Brague, "L'image et l'acédie", *Revue Thomiste* 85 (1985): 197–228, at 204: "The devil prevents the eclipse of the sun, which seems hopelessly stationary. But he suggests that charity, instead, 'has been eclipsed'."

[31] Ibid.

When I want to rest my heart, fatigued by the darkness which surrounds it by the memory of the luminous country after which I aspire, my torment redoubles; it seems to me that the darkness, borrowing the voice of sinners, says mockingly to me: "You are dreaming about the light, about a fatherland embalmed in the sweetest perfumes; you are dreaming about the *eternal possession* of the Creator of all these marvels; you believe that one day you will walk out of this fog which surrounds you! Advance, advance; rejoice in death which will give you not what you hope for but a night still more profound, the night of nothingness."[32]

But this is also a temptation that awaits us all, whoever we may be:

We meet materialists who make such peremptory statements about the meaning of life that they shake our certitudes. There are people who have no spiritual concerns yet are so content that they seem obviously to be in the right. To put it bluntly, our hope in invisible goods seems like a myth. Everything is called into question. Are we dupes? This temptation is more dangerous than impure thoughts![33]

But if doubt is a temptation of the devil, it is more particularly the temptation of the *noonday* devil. Indeed, since it is the midday devil, it is also the devil of the "mid-life crisis", in other words, of the turning point in life. It awaits us, however, at any moment, even though it certainly attacks more violently toward the middle of life, at a mature age, when it is too late to "do one's life over". People often

---

[32] Thérèse of the Child Jesus, Manuscript C, in *Story of a Soul*, trans. John Clarke, O.C.D. (Washington, D.C.: ICS Publications, 1975), 213.

[33] Père Jérôme, *Tout à Dieu* (Saint-Maur: Parole et Silence, 1998), 13.

talk in this sense about the "crisis of their forties" or of their fifties, and rightly so. Just as at noon one assesses the morning, so too at that age one is already making a kind of assessment of one's life. Could it not be time to set off in a new direction? Have I done right in committing myself to this path?

So it is that acedia is above all the devil who causes us to regret the decision that we have made. This is the sense in which it is the devil of maturity, even though one may still be young. Whereas there is one devil who keeps man from making a commitment, from taking a step, acedia makes him regret having taken it. So we see the paradox of flight: while it seems to be an advance, it is instead a genuine regression. One might say that it is a retreat, or even a "flight backward". But it is not always possible to flee! The only safe path then becomes mediocrity.

Mediocrity

Scripture warns us severely: "So because you are luke-warm, and neither cold nor hot, I will spew you out of my mouth" (Rev 3:16). This is indeed what the passage is about. If the modern era has reduced acedia to a sort of lukewarmness, it is clearly because negligence and medi-ocrity are real elements of it, even though we cannot re-duce it to that. When it seems too late to make a new start, to do one's life over, only one solution remains: to live in mediocrity.

A person then begins to become neglectful about little things. Minor, almost imperceptible infidelities crop up.

Then, one fine day, he notices—or rather, other people notice, since the devil of acedia does everything he can to remain unknown to the person he is attacking—that he has strayed from the path, that he has lost his way.

> When infidelity becomes blatant and manifest, let us not be scandalized; instead, let us remember how it began. It is usually the result of insignificant little everyday infidelities; these infidelities gave rise to doubt, which, in turn, produced sadness, boredom, then indifference, and finally anxiety and acedia, which, sooner or later, burst forth.[34]

Such negligence reveals a lack of faith in the dignity of human action performed in the Spirit. Indeed, when someone no longer dares to do what is essential and great, one must be content with what is secondary and mediocre.

In order to flee mediocrity and be faithful to the sublime vocation to which man is called—to become a saint, to have a share in the divine life—it is necessary to remain faithful in the little things. Indeed, the trial itself can be a reason for hope:

> Knowing well our human weakness, the Lord exhorted us to be faithful in very little things (Lk 16:10; 19:17; Mt 25:21), because the trials that will arrive must by no means be experienced as burdens, but must be faced as opportunities for perseverance and tested fidelity and, therefore, as reasons for hope.[35]

It is necessary to be able to live the present moment intensely, knowing that it is an opportunity to encounter the Lord. To flee mediocrity is therefore to persevere on

---

[34] E. Bianchi, *Le manteau d'Elie*, VM 25 (Bégrolles-en-Mauges: Bellefontaine, 1991), 113–14.

[35] Ibid., 114.

the narrow way that leads to salvation, instead of setting out on the wide, easy way that ultimately leads to perdition (Mt 7:13); it is to reject compromise and to choose holiness.

> The devil's tactic is to propose what is "reasonable". . . . Yes, he is the prince of lukewarmness, the king of compromise. His goal is not to make us fall into specific errors but, on the contrary, to leave us in uncertainty, to submerge truth in uncertainty. Because it is impossible to stake one's life on vague ideas and, consequently, to become a saint under those conditions.[36]

Distraction and compensations

Distraction is the corollary of instability. No doubt you remember how Saint Thomas showed that acedia provoked a twofold movement: first a movement of flight from what causes the sadness or disgust; then a second movement of active seeking: the search for compensations, distractions. Every man can be subject to the test of time and, therefore, to the trial of boredom; boredom that is not only a passing, external phenomenon but in the end reveals a profound incapacity of the will. That is when someone may choose to be distracted, to "amuse oneself", by seeking compensations or else by falling into activism.

> One seeks, not fullness, but rather the accumulation of images as an evasion. Travel agencies proliferate. No one thinks of anything but getting away, but wherever he goes, he takes himself along. Now if emptiness, anxiety, boredom dwell within a being, this emptiness, anxiety, and boredom will follow him to the ends of the earth. The

[36] M.-D. Molinié, "Du désespoir à l'adoration", 10.

tenacious illusion of always being better off elsewhere does not abandon the individual. Anything seems preferable to self-awareness and diffuse pain.[37]

When we addressed the problem of *sense*, a little earlier, we spoke about orientation and meaning. But the word "sense" also denotes the body's faculty of perceiving realities outside itself: meaning and sensation are therefore closely connected.[38] Hence we can understand how acedia, because it attacks the meaning of life, can also drive the senses to distraction: "If we cannot keep meaning, then at least let us not lose sensations!" the devil of acedia seems to murmur.

> Anything, rather than a lack of sensations! To the point where someone goes so far as to want to have worries, so as to get over his boredom! To the point that someone seeks to reactivate the pleasurable sensations experienced in early childhood: for example, those of the oral stage, which lead one to eat or drink excessively. To the point that someone begins to have psychosomatic symptoms; bodily ills take the place of words.[39]

So we see the reappearance, in all of their splendor, of the different daughters of acedia mentioned by Saint Thomas Aquinas; they have lost none of their relevance and only cause us to conform to the world:

—*mental flightiness*: since man has lost the inexhaustible surprise of Divine Love, he is seized by a frenzy for novelty. The multiple pursuits that present themselves to my mind attract me, solely because they deliver me

[37] See I. Prêtre, *La tentation du désespoir*, Sagesse (Paris: Médiaspaul, 1996), 87.
[38] Thévenot, *Avance en eau profonde!*, 45: "Nothing makes sense unless it is first perceived by the senses."
[39] Ibid.

from what I ought to do at this precise moment! Now what is asked of me, on the contrary, is to be able to rediscover the spiritual motivation of action, regardless of the dignity of this or that particular action: the present activity is the place of my encounter with God; it must not be abandoned.

— *garrulousness*: man flees thought so as to take refuge in speech; and *curiosity*: since he has lost his perspective on eternity, he compensates by a perpetual search for substitutes. Saint Paul had already painted a realistic portrait of these two defects in describing young widows (cf. 1 Tim 5:13). Such garrulousness and such curiosity about other people's business are the sign of a lack of substance in one's own personal life. While focused very often on the faults of others, these gossips become set in their own mediocrity.

— *physical agitation*: Saint Thomas saw in this the inability of the body to remain in the same place. This psychological insight is rather shrewd: certain forms of bodily agitation may manifest an uncontrollable nervousness of the soul. We can classify here also the constant tendency to consider most attractive those pursuits that take one far from home or from one's city. Here again we find the last daughter of acedia, *instability*, who thinks that by changing where one is, one can change who one is.

— another way of fleeing, finally, is *activism*. This resembles the physical agitation that we just discussed. The latter, indeed, is not limited to the body's inability to stay in one place; it can also be a disordered activism that leads to inventing constantly new things to do. Despite a great deal of activity, this activism paradoxically is combined with torpor and dejection, for it too is a flight that is supposed to make up for the dread of nothingness. In confronting this activism, should we not rediscover the meaning of fasting, which is openness and availability? Now, the detachment of fasting can be applied to areas other than food: the area of activity, for example. This can therefore be the opportunity to rediscover Sunday, the Lord's day, and time given freely to God.

> So it is that we can seek in activism and overworking a secret pleasure, as though we needed to cram our schedules full in order to have the feeling of being alive. Time free of a useful, profitable occupation makes us uneasy; therefore we fill it up so as to dispel the anxiety of emptiness. . . . To agree to devote time to something gratuitous—prayer, spiritual reading, friendship—helps us to let go of the illusion that we control our lives and enables us to wait humbly and confidently for God's gift: this is the meaning of the Jewish Sabbath and the Christian Sunday, which punctuate each week by reminding man that his work does not find its accomplishment in itself but, rather, awaits it from God; once his work is done, man is called to open himself up to praise and thanksgiving.[40]

Joyful Perseverance

Finally, the strategy to be deployed against the devil of acedia can be summarized in the phrase: joyful perseverance. This is perhaps the expression that best synthesizes the set of methods to be applied in fighting against acedia. One of the dangers of acedia is that it seems to be without any

---

[40] É. Ricaud, "Pourquoi l'ascèse?", *Sources Vives* 84 (1999): 22–23.

apparent cause. This is not a sadness due to a particular suffering or to the absence of a specific good. It is a drop in the soul's potential and involves the life of the Christian in terms of its own dynamism: it corresponds to a sort of blockage, a break in the search for God. In this sense we can say that it is the moral trial par excellence. Hence there is no well-defined strategy for the battle: everything can be summed up in this word: perseverance!

Standing fast

Evagrius and the Desert Fathers traced all remedies back to just one, as we saw: perseverance (*hypomonē*).

> The ancient masters of the spiritual life recognized one remedy above all others against the *hopelessness* that we call *acedia*. That remedy is long-suffering, patience, *hypomonē* in its literal sense of abiding beneath the yoke.[41]

Then it will be a question of focusing one's efforts, depending on the various forms taken by the flight from self or from God. Therefore it is necessary to resist, to stand fast, to persevere, to remain faithful. All these expressions manifest the battle against *wandering thoughts*, that flight which takes us not only outside our cell but also outside of time, outside of our state of life, and finally outside of our condition as creatures. Acedia is the temptation to withdraw from the narrowness of the present so as to take refuge in what is imaginary; it is the temptation to quit the battle so as to become a simple spectator of the controversy that is unfolding in the world.

[41] C. Schönborn, *Loving the Church: Retreat to John Paul II and the Papal Household* (San Francisco: Ignatius Press, 1998), 161–62.

Now the Fathers were very realistic: well they knew that the solution is not to abandon the combat, to leave our narrow dwelling, but, rather, to raise our eyes toward heaven, toward Him who waits to see us fight.[42] For he who goes out, thinking that he is freeing himself from what seems to him like a prison, in reality falls back into a snare and even more solid fetters: the prison and slavery of sin.

Stability in our own place

Ultimately, though, what then is the place that we should not abandon at any cost? What is the place in which we should observe stability? G. Angelini proposed two interpretations of this proper "place" in which it is necessary to stand fast:

—our dwelling place is first of all our *profound desire*, the desire that is in us even before we are conscious of it, before we even become conscious of ourselves:[43] it is the *desiderium* about which we said that it was a movement tending toward the *gaudium* [joy] of possessing the final end, which is real union with the beloved. But we saw also the close connection that exists between the desire for the final end and hope: acedia is precisely a sin against hope, inasmuch as it is opposed to the *desiderium* of beatitude. If the desire can be considered our dwelling place, then this is true insofar as it becomes a virtue. When the desire concerns the *end*, it must become *hope*;

---

[42] Athanasius, *Life of Antony*, 10, 3 (NPNF-2 4:199a): "Antony, I was here, but I waited to see thy fight."

[43] G. Angelini, *Le virtù e la fede* (Milan: Glossa, 1994), 66.

when it concerns *the means to the end*, it must become *temperance.*

—our dwelling place, Angelini again explains, is also the place that God assigned to our life and that we ourselves have recognized and chosen at the moments of greatest clarity in our life; in other words: our own vocation, our specific calling.[44] Acedia manifests itself, then, as the temptation to deny our commitment, our choice of life. We see here how the spatial dimension and the temporal dimension of acedia combine in the danger of infidelity to a commitment that has been made.

To observe stability, on the contrary, is for us the way to avoid falling into *utopia*, which literally means finding oneself "nowhere". Sometimes a person in the grip of acedia has the feeling that perseverance in his own "place" is only hypocrisy or falsehood. "What good is it to stay," he tells himself, "if I no longer believe in it? It is a lack of honesty on my part; I would do better to leave!" In reality, such a thought is not fair; it is characterized by an unrealistic sentimentality. The fact that I no longer "feel" anything today in no way calls into question the commitment that I made yesterday! Indeed, in the sight of God, the commitment can only be definitive, because God always remains faithful.

This is demonstrated by the beautiful account of the covenant between God and Abraham in chapter 15 of the Book of Genesis. Abraham takes the animals, cuts them in

[44] Ibid., 67–71.

two, and places each half opposite the other. Then he falls into a mysterious sleep, like Adam during the creation [of Eve], or like Christ on the Cross. It is a scriptural way of saying that God has the initiative. Now, during this sleep, God passes between these pieces, making a "round trip", so to speak. In the ancient Near East, when a covenant was made, each of the two parties walked between pieces of animals that had been quartered. But with God, it is not like that. Only God passes through, and he makes a "round trip", in other words, he passes once for himself and once for Abraham. God knows very well that Abraham, left to his own devices, cannot remain faithful to the covenant. So God commits himself for Abraham.

This magnificent account should fill us, too, with hope: God committed himself in the covenant "in our place", in other words, for us. He is the one who will enable us to remain faithful. Without him, we could not do it. This is also what Saint Paul tells Timothy: "If we are faithless, he remains faithful—for he cannot deny himself" (2 Tim 2:13). Therefore the Christian can be faithful to his baptismal promises; the Christian committed to a particular state of life can be faithful to his commitment, which was made in complete freedom and authenticated by the Church.

But such perseverance requires confident abandonment to God's plan for me. There is a love that precedes me and calls me; this love will never die, and I rely on it in order to remain faithful. Now this "abode of fidelity"[45] is not somewhere else; on the contrary, it is precisely here where I find myself, at this moment. Therefore an attitude

[45] See Hans Urs von Balthasar, "La demeure de la fidélité", *Communio* I/4 (1976): 2–14.

of faith is what is demanded of me: faith in a God who calls me by my name and who leads me himself, if I do not refuse to entrust my life to him.

There is still another proper "place" in which we must remain joyfully: the Church. Acedia, indeed, can manifest itself as the temptation to leave the Church. How many Christians do not feel right in the Church? How many of them think that the Church is "behind the times", that she has remained in the Middle Ages, and wish that she would catch up with the modern era? They wonder why she does not develop more quickly by conforming to the world to which she is supposed to bring the Good News. They wonder also what authority the Church could have when she makes pronouncements about questions involving an area in which she is not an expert. What right does she have, for example, to meddle in matters with regard to the beginnings of human life, or, on the contrary, those that concern its final moments? Others, on the other hand, think that the Church took a wrong turn, that she is no longer faithful to the precepts of her Lord. But if someone judges the Church and her Magisterium in this way, is he not putting himself "above" her or outside her? If the Christian finds himself too constrained in the Church, is it not because, ultimately, he is too constrained in his own heart?

Let us never forget that the Church is the Body of Christ and therefore the essential place of Christian action, the activity that unfolds in space and time under the direction of the Holy Spirit. The Holy Spirit prompts the Christian interiorly and grants that he may already anticipate, in his acts, the definitive encounter in the eternal abode: the Father's house. Now here below, action itself has an abode, and this dwelling place is the Church. Therefore the Church is where we will attain the true freedom of the children of God, according to the remark that Saint Augustine commends to us for the days of acedia: "Do not go looking for a liberation which will lead you far from the house of your liberator!"[46]

It is also necessary to rediscover the beauty of forgiveness, both given and received, as an excellent act that participates in Christ's action. The Christian's action will thus become the place of his communion with Christ, the source of communion among men. Furthermore, if we have succumbed to the temptation to flee, forgiveness enables us to return to our house, where the Father will be there with open arms to welcome us: "It was fitting to make merry and be glad, for this your brother was dead, and is alive; he was lost, and is found" (Lk 15:32). Having returned to his ecclesial abode, the Christian is once again fully reintegrated into the community of the children of God and thereby a sharer in the divine circulation of the sap of life and bearing fruit for the salvation of the world (Jn 15:5).

Remembering

One appeal resounds throughout Scripture: "Do not forget!" The Book of Deuteronomy, in particular, is filled with these urgent appeals.[47] God asks his people not to for-

---

[46] Saint Augustine, *Enarratio in Psalmum XCIX*, 7 (CCL 39:1397), cited by John Paul II, encyclical *Veritatis splendor* (August 6, 1993), no. 87.

[47] See, for example, Deut 4:9, 23; 6:12; 8:11; 9:7.

get his benefits, his salvific intervention in history of Israel. What, then, does acedia have to do with memory? Maybe more than one might think at first glance. Indeed, if the Christian is tempted to abandon his own place, the place of his specific calling, it is because he no longer remembers the quality of the motives that led him, earlier, to make this or that fundamental choice. In this sense, no doubt, we can speak about acedia as a "sin against memory".

It is therefore essential to remember, to recall the marvels that God has accomplished in history, but also in *my* personal history, above all to recall Christ Jesus, and to do so in the routine of everyday life. Here it is necessary to mention the Eucharistic Memorial, which is not just the memory of a deed from the past but is truly the representation of Christ's sacrifice, for love of mankind, in an eschatological perspective: "As often as you eat this bread and drink the chalice, you proclaim the Lord's death until he comes" (1 Cor 11:26).

There is an essential dimension of temporality in the Eucharist. The Eucharistic Sacrifice, renewed unceasingly, is however the opposite of a boring repetition; on the contrary, it manifests the eternal fidelity of God, who demands in return man's fidelity, the unconditional gift of himself while he is subject to the trials of time.

Jesus Christ chose the most repetitive, commonplace gesture, eating and drinking, the most necessary and most modest means of sustaining life, bread and wine, in order to hide within them the most unheard-of, most meaningful and purposeful act, the only one capable of extending history beyond death: love to the end, the gift of self even unto the Cross. He thus commits the unique event of his

Passover, the Hour of all hours, to everyday routine in the sacramental repetition. The breaking of the bread becomes, for the duration of history, the Eucharistic Memorial.[48]

The Eucharist is what gives temporality its ultimate meaning, since it takes up the past, the present, and the future: love never passes away (1 Cor 13:8):

Our individual death and all the deaths in history do not reduce the passage of time to absurdity, nor do they make its course undifferentiated. They themselves are taken up into the Eucharistic Memorial that has already assumed them and offered them and that one day will transfigure them into the fullness of life. It is enough to recall how forcefully the Eucharistic anamnesis interconnects the past, the present, and the future to understand how decisively the Church's liturgy is the guardian of the meaning of temporality: "When we eat this bread and drink this cup, we celebrate the mystery of faith: we *recall* your death, O risen Lord, and we *await* your coming."[49]

There is a close connection between Eucharistic Memorial and moral action: the Eucharist supports the action with its presence, enlivens it with its sacrifice, and nourishes it with communion.

Joy of heart: an unerring criterion

"Restore to me the joy of your salvation, and uphold me with a willing spirit" (Ps 51:12). This is the prayer that must dwell in our hearts on days of acedia. It sums up perfectly our spiritual attitude when confronted by temptation. We are radically saved, restored to life with Christ:

[48] Léna, "Éloge du temps ordinaire", 23.
[49] Ibid., 26.

our sadness has definitively been changed into joy (Jn 16:20).[50] This *gaudium* resulting from the Resurrection of Christ is something that we must show; we must witness to it. We are called to a marvelous work: to help others —to the meager extent that we can, in other words, by our excellent actions—to walk toward our perfect fulfillment in Christ. Now this requires magnanimity, greatness of soul.

Joy is clearly the unerring criterion, the spiritual barometer that directs us concerning our spiritual life. A Carthusian monk understood this perfectly: "Sadness is looking at oneself; joy is looking at God."[51] This joy is *gaudium*, fruit of communion with a personal being. It is the anticipation, in faith, of the full and definitive union with the God of Love.

> Communion with truth, with grandeur, with beauty, with other spiritual persons—there is the innermost heart of man. This is the plenitude, at once tranquilizing and exalting, to which he always aspires, often enough without knowing it. If there is joy in successful effort, there is a greater in realized communion. And it is because it achieves the deepest of communions, the communion of living persons with each other, that love is the unparalleled force it is, and source of a joy that does not pass.[52]

Recent popes have often insisted on the importance of joy and the fact that it is an unerring criterion. Reflect

[50] The joy of the Resurrection is a spiritual joy; it is truly *gaudium*, as Christ declares in John 16:20: "Your sorrow will turn into joy" (Tristitia vestra convertetur in gaudium).

[51] Dom A. Guillerand, *Écrits spirituels* (Rome: Benedittine di Priscilla, 1966), 2:226.

[52] Jean Mouroux, *The Meaning of Man* (New York: Sheed & Ward, 1948), 4.

on these words of John Paul II on the eve of the year 2000:

> *The term "Jubilee" speaks of joy;* not just an inner joy but a jubilation which is manifested outwardly, for the coming of God is also an outward, visible, audible and tangible event, as Saint John makes clear (cf. 1 Jn 1:1). It is thus appropriate that every sign of joy at this coming should have its own outward expression. This will demonstrate that *the Church rejoices in salvation.* She invites everyone to rejoice, and she tries to create conditions to ensure that the power of salvation may be shared by all.[53]

As for Pope Benedict XVI, he has not stopped appealing to joy, to the point where it has been said that the invitation to joy is an interpretive key to all his theology.[54] Let us quote just one short text, among so many others, that insists on the specific character of spiritual joy, *gaudium,* as distinct from pleasure, as Saint Thomas analyzed it so well.

> Once again, it is necessary to make it clear that pleasure is not everything. May Christianity give us joy, just as love gives joy. But love is always also a renunciation of self. The Lord himself has given us the formula of what love is: those who lose themselves find themselves; those who spare or save themselves are lost. It is always an "Exodus", hence, painful. True joy is something different from pleasure; joy grows and continues to mature in suffering, in communion with the Cross of Christ. It is here alone that the true joy of faith is born.[55]

[53] John Paul II, apostolic letter *Tertio millennio adveniente* (November 10, 1944), 16.

[54] See the beautiful book by J. Murphy, *Christ Our Joy: The Theological Vision of Pope Benedict XVI* (San Francisco: Ignatius Press, 2008), especially pp. 31–36, which discuss acedia.

[55] Benedict XVI, Address to the Diocesan Clergy of Aosta (July 25, 2005).

Finally we quote a passage from Pope Francis, who also, from the very beginning of his pontificate, has been pleased to invite the faithful to joy, by relating it moreover to the Cross:

> And here the first word that I wish to say to you: *joy!* Do not be men and women of sadness: a Christian can never be sad! Never give way to discouragement! Ours is not a joy born of having many possessions, but from having encountered a Person: Jesus, in our midst; it is born from knowing that with him we are never alone, even at difficult moments, even when our life's journey comes up against problems and obstacles that seem insurmountable, and there are so many of them! And in this moment the enemy, the devil, comes, often disguised as an angel, and slyly speaks his word to us. Do not listen to him! Let us follow Jesus! We accompany, we follow Jesus, but above all we know that he accompanies us and carries us on his shoulders. This is our joy, this is the hope that we must bring to this world. Please do not let yourselves be robbed of hope! Do not let hope be stolen! The hope that Jesus gives us. . . . Christ's Cross embraced with love never leads to sadness, but to joy, to the joy of having been saved and of doing a little of what he did on the day of his death.[56]

Although acedia is the sin opposed to joy, to *gaudium*, nevertheless, in comparison with all other sins, it has the advantage of not being followed immediately by any other thought; on the contrary, Evagrius tells us, after the fight comes a state of extraordinary peace and an inexpressible joy.[57] This is also the joy Saint Antony experienced when he conquered acedia.

---

[56] Pope Francis, homily, Palm Sunday (March 24, 2013).
[57] Evagrius, *Praktikos* 12, p. 99.

It was an angel of the Lord sent to correct Antony and to make him vigilant. He heard the voice of the angel saying, "Do this and you will be cured." When he heard it he was very glad and recovered his confidence. He did what the angel had done, and found the salvation that he was seeking.[58]

Finally, although it is a sin against *gaudium*, acedia leads nevertheless to it, if the individual has been able to resist it and remain faithful. Then, the soul that has persevered will hear the Lord tell him: "Well done, good and faithful servant. . . . Enter into the joy of your master!" (Mt 25:21). And it is remarkable that the word "joy" (*gaudium*) here designates, without a doubt, an "abode": the servant enters into this joy, as he enters into the eternal dwelling place of the Father. Although acedia, a sin against joy, causes us to leave our true abode, the fidelity received from God enables us to enter into the dwelling place of God, into his own joy.

[58] *Apophtegme Antoine* 1 (SC 387:336); English trans. in *The Desert Fathers: Sayings of the Early Christian Monks*, trans. and with an introduction by Benedicta Ward (London: Penguin Books, 2003), 60.

4

Acedia in the Different
States of Life

You are no doubt wondering what could still be added to these pages! True, we have already said a lot of things about acedia and its relevance in our lives! We have seen that it poses the supreme threat of the disintegration of the human person; we discussed in detail the two dimensions of it, spatial and temporal, in our daily lives; we called for a rediscovery of the joy of being saved.

However, it would be interesting, in this final chapter, to present the specific forms that acedia can assume in the different states of life of a Christian. Specifically, I will focus on three states of life: monastic life, priestly life, and married life, without neglecting a few remarks about single people.

Acedia in Religious Life Today

The first state that I would like to discuss is consecrated life, as it is experienced specifically in monastic life. No doubt this is practically the only setting in which people still speak about acedia nowadays and still have some idea of what it is about. But let us be honest: Even in the monastery, is not acedia often considered something a bit outmoded? Certainly, when the monks and nuns were novices they read the descriptions by Evagrius and Cassian, but the novitiate is over and has been for a long time! Now perhaps precisely because the novitiate is a distant memory, along with its fervent ardor, the devil of acedia can attack more effectively. So let us see for ourselves.

To go out, at all costs . . .

If the first manifestation of acedia, for the ancients, was the felt need to go out of one's cell, that must still be the case today. The little cell in which the monk spends his whole day can become in the long run, understandably, almost unbearable. Hence the feeling of profound aversion for the place where he finds himself. However, as we have already suggested, the temptation to wander about physically is the tangible manifestation of a more fundamental evil that threatens the whole spiritual life: *instability*. Finally, what the vagabond monk is fleeing is himself, and, thereby, God.

> The flight from self is concealed beneath the flight from one's setting and way of life. It will be better elsewhere; it used to be better back then. In short, the here and now become unbearable. Alone and confronting himself, beneath the noonday sun, the monk can no longer see or hear himself; he no longer tolerates himself. His illusory salvation lies in desertion.[1]

This feeling of instability is inappropriate in the life of a hermit. In monastic life, too, perseverance in one's cell is not always easy, even though it is less radical than for recluses. Evagrius' humorous description has lost none of its relevance for some monks of the twenty-first century.

---

[1] É. Junod, *Les sages du désert: Antoine, Pachrôme, Évagre, Syméa* (Geneva: Labor et fides, 1991), 81.

And yet the cell is the sanctuary where each monk encounters his God in silence, for personal prayer and *lectio divina*. It is the prolongation of the monastery church where the community liturgy is celebrated: there the monk prolongs the prayer in choir through an intimate heart-to-heart with the Lord who has led him to the desert.

> An old man said: "The cell of the monk is the furnace in Babylon, where the three young men found the Son of God: and it is also the pillar of cloud from which God spoke to Moses."[2]

But this difficulty staying in one's cell, of course, applies also to perseverance in the monastery itself, especially for monks or nuns living in community. Here again, there is no lack of pretexts for requesting an outing: concern for one's family, a charitable visit, a well-deserved rest . . . To say nothing of the impression of literally suffocating within the monastery precincts. Evagrius had already unmasked all these excuses in the fourth century! With regard to this temptation, monastic tradition is explicit: without perseverance in a place, no spiritual fruit is possible.

> An old man said: "Even as a tree cannot bear fruit if it be often transplanted, no more can a monk that is often removing from one place to another."[3]

This is why Saint Benedict insists so much on stability in the monastery: it is the workshop in which one wields the tools of the spiritual art (*Rule of St. Benedict* 4, 75). This is why arrangements should be made so that everything

---

[2] *The Sayings of the Fathers*, translated from the Greek by Pelagius the Deacon and John the Subdeacon, VII, 38, in *The Desert Fathers*, trans. Helen Waddell (New York: Henry Holt, 1936), pp. 79–178 at 123.

[3] Ibid., VII, 36, p. 123.

necessary is found inside the monastery, so that the monks do not need to leave it—something that is by no means beneficial to their souls (*RB* 66, 6). Saint Benedict had clearly understood that the reason why the monk has withdrawn from the world is to belong to God alone at the heart of the world.[4] Now in order to do that, he has to be rooted in a geographical place and in a community; what is necessary is not exterior scattering but the preservation of internal unity. This is the indispensable condition for safeguarding the spiritual life.

> Syncletica said: "If you live in a monastic community, do not wander from place to place; if you do, it will harm you. If a hen stops sitting on the eggs she will hatch no chickens. The monk or nun who goes from place to place grows cold and dead in faith."[5]

To remain at all costs is certainly the appropriate remedy, even today, according to the unanimous teaching of the Fathers. Listen to this:

> A brother was in the desert and practiced *hesychia* in his cell. Acedia tormented him cruelly to make him leave it, but he said to himself: "Why this acedia, unhappy wretch? Why do you seek to go out of your cell? Even if you do nothing good, is it not enough for you not to scandalize and bother anyone, and also not to be scandalized or bothered yourself by anyone?" . . . Whenever the brother said these or similar things to himself, a great consolation came over him

---

[4] The Vatican II decree *Perfectae caritatis* recalls this: "The principal duty of monks is to offer a service to the divine majesty at once humble and noble within the walls of the monastery" (PC 7).

[5] *Synclétique* 6 (SC 387:350); English trans. in *The Desert Fathers: Sayings of the Early Christian Monks*, trans. and with an introduction by Benedicta Ward (London: Penguin Books, 2003), 63.

by the grace of God. He had received this teaching from the saintly fathers who had grown old in the desert and by their asceticism enjoyed great familiarity with God.[6]

The ancients knew very well indeed that flight is no solution; on the contrary, it would only increase the evil, as Cassian says very clearly.

> The wretched soul . . . [is] weakened the more by this remedy which it seeks for the present. For the more frequently and more severely will the enemy attack one who, when the battle is joined, will as he well knows immediately turn his back, and whom he sees to look for safety neither in victory nor in fighting but in flight.[7]

Certainly, although temptations lie in wait for all men, they are no doubt even more intense in the case of a monk, who according to all of monastic tradition is a "wrestler". It is precisely from his manner of struggling that he will be recognized as a monk.[8] Often, when thoughts wage war against us, there is no other way to fight than physical perseverance.

> A certain brother who was tormented by his thoughts urging him to leave the monastery, told it to the abbot. And he said, "Go, and sit down, and give thy body in pledge to the wall of thy cell, and go not out thence: but let thy thought go: let it think as much as it likes, provided thou fling not thy body out of the cell."[9]

---

[6] *Apophtegme* PE III, 13, 8 (*Les Sentences des Pères du désert: Collection alphabétique* (Solesmes: Éditions de Solesmes, 1981), 2:183).

[7] John Cassian, *Institutes* X, 3 (NPNF-2 11:267b).

[8] *Poemen* 13 (SC 387:350): English trans. in *Desert Fathers: Sayings*, 63. "Poemen said, 'The character of the genuine monk only appears when he is tempted.'"

[9] *Sayings of the Fathers*, VII, 37, p. 123.

This, however, does not dispense a monk from interior vigilance, because he may be deluded into thinking that he is serving God just because he remains silent, while his interior thoughts murmur incessantly. The ancients knew too that one way of overcoming acedia is to ridicule it by continually postponing flight until later; this is how one manages to remain faithful for one's whole life!

> It was said of Abba Theodore and Abba Lucius, both from Ennaton, that they spent fifty years ridiculing their own thoughts by saying: "After this winter we will depart from here." And when summer returned, they would say, "After this summer, we will depart from here." And that is what they did their whole life long, those memorable Fathers.[10]

For in the final analysis, what must be changed is not one's place, but rather one's heart: it is necessary to convert.

The interior void

Let us go a little farther. The temptation to flee is not simply a transient wish. Sometimes it seems that it is a genuine necessity: you cannot take it any more! Evagrius spoke about a "relaxation" of the soul and a "burdensome" sadness. In those who have left the world for the spiritual combat of the desert, this feeling can become extraordinarily acute.

> The devil of acedia starts by making the soul feel the weight of time; the day seems just endless. Then the victim, prey to a sentiment of emptiness, can no longer concentrate. He waits for it to end, hoping that someone will come to lend some substance to that day. But nothing and no one comes

[10] *Théodore de l'Ennaton* (SC 387:342).

to fill that void. Besides, who could fill it, since it is interior?[11]

The monk has left for the desert, or for the monastery, in order to be saved, and now that is precisely what seems impossible. Saint Antony utters a heart-wrenching cry: "Lord, I want to be made whole and my thoughts do not let me."[12] However, temptation is precisely an anticipation of victory, since it is aroused by the desire for salvation. An inherent part of the monk's condition is to be subject to trials:

> The search for salvation is just what drives the monk to the desert, the place where temptation becomes extremely dangerous. Therefore the will to be saved is what arouses tribulation. It does not make it out of whole cloth; rather, it brings to the surface the permanent nature of the Christian way of being present in the world. Temptation makes the monk's very status in the world appear to be tribulation.[13]

The oppression is such that it annihilates all the strength of the individual, leaving him exhausted, that is to say, emptied. This is exactly the sensation that is experienced: total emptiness. It can even go farther: there is the danger of falling into the abyss of nothingness, one might say: into a certain "atheism". But is not nothingness precisely what the God of love chose in order to be reunited with his creature? "Though he was in the form of God, [Jesus] did not count equality with God a thing to be grasped, but *emptied himself*, taking the form of a servant, being born in

[11] É. Junod, *Les sages du désert*, 81.
[12] *Antoine* I (SC 387:336); English trans. in *Desert Fathers: Sayings*, 60.
[13] Rémi Brague, "L'image et l'acédie", *Revue Thomiste* 85 (1985): 215.

the likeness of men. And being found in human form he humbled himself and became obedient unto death, even death on a cross" (Phil 2:6–8).

The monk, too, must "empty himself ", no doubt more than anyone else, so as to leave the entire space for the Interior Guest. This is precisely the meaning of his asceticism: to attain purity of heart, simplicity of heart, the integration of his whole being.

> This may seem paradoxical: How is it possible to be tempt-ed by atheism in a life of seeking God? And yet, this is the greatest temptation for a monk of mature age. In a life punctuated by prayer, consecrated to the service of God, he runs the risk of being tempted by atheism. Not by the ideological atheism of the world, but by a much more sub-tle kind: the atheism of nothingness. . . . By dint of con-tinually renouncing everything so as to seek God alone, he [the monk] may find himself facing the abyss of nothing-ness, the void of atheism! After he has shut many doors or allowed others to close them behind him, suddenly the door of atheism may open wide before him.[14]

Now emptiness is also the simplicity of unity, the sim-plicity of the exclusive search for the Absolute. One mean-ing of the word "monk" (in Greek *monos*) is precisely this: someone who is progressively unified, someone who be-comes "one", because he has only one desire left: God.

> To become more and more unified—that is something al-together concrete, since we are so occupied and even torn asunder by many desires. The monk's path will be to con-sent, little by little, to the passage of all his desires—and

[14] E. Bianchi, *Le manteau d'Elie*, VM 25 (Bégrolles-en-Mauges: Bellefon-taine, 1991), 102.

we would no longer be human if we ceased to desire—into the crucible of the one and only true desire: God.[15]

But this is a frightening process: people often prefer the dispersion of multiplicity to interior unity. This is why another manifestation of monastic acedia will be the search for compensations.

The search for compensations

On the day of his final profession, the monk gave everything: he no longer has the use of his goods or that of his body or that of his will. But when God no longer suffices, there is a great temptation to take back subtly what one has given away once and for all. If one has totally lost a taste for spiritual things, it can even happen that one is practically unaware of it: when spiritual joy is gone, with it goes the judgment by way of connaturality with which "the spiritual man judges all things" (1 Cor 2:15).

> There is a temptation, for each one of us, to take back our marbles, to reclaim, openly or more subtly, what we renounced in becoming monks. For Saint Benedict, things are our worst enemies, because, in offering us a certain autonomy, they invite us to abandon the "difficult, harsh" things that lead to God. That is why Saint Benedict chose to cut off temptations at the root, by forbidding any return to "the onions of Egypt" (see Num 11:5), for our freedom consists, not in always being able to turn back, but rather in being able to weather the storms.[16]

---

[15] J. Chauvelot, *Citoyen du ciel, citoyen du monde* (Montrouge: Bayard, 2011), 41.

[16] G. Jedrzejczak, *Sur un chemin de liberté* (Montreal: Anne Sigier, 2006), 395.

Usually the monk afflicted with acedia will find compensations outside of the monastery: emotional compensations, the repeated search for contacts with the outside, various commitments in associations or groups. When Saint Benedict speaks about the world, he does so positively. To welcome someone who knocks at the door is to welcome Christ in person. However, Benedict insists that the monastery be organized in such a way that the monk is not obliged to go out. Indeed, what is bad is not the world but the tendency that we have to spread ourselves thin, to scatter ourselves outside.

> Monastic enclosure is in the first place this: this awareness of our poverty, our limits, and our weakness, which prevent us from finding the paths of our own heart and drive us to seek outside, in relations, friendships, and so on, what we gave up seeking within.[17]

These compensations manifest themselves also through little failings in the practice of poverty, fasting, silence, obedience: insignificant failings, at the start, which gradually intensify, without the monk even realizing it, if he is not very vigilant. Since community life is ultimately very demanding, acedia drives him to individualism: instead of taking advantage of the moments provided for community exchanges, he isolates himself from the brethren and seeks elsewhere what he has excluded himself from. He then ends up constructing for himself his own little life, "without care" (a-kèdia) about the others. Moreover, he soothes his conscience by telling himself that he is not

[17] Ibid., 437.

disturbing anyone . . . But is he not disturbing God and the plan of love that he had for us?

This is why, given the temptation to seek compensations, it is necessary to renew one's vigilance in little things. The adversary's intention is to put the monk's resolve to the test: the latter must therefore adapt to his tactics by anticipating him on occasion: he will rise a little earlier for the Divine Office; he will be able to do without an object before becoming attached to it or to break off a relationship before it captures his heart; he will be capable of rendering service voluntarily before it is asked of him; he will develop the habit of completing with the utmost care a work that he would prefer to finish as quickly as possible, and so on. This is a practical wisdom that Evagrius had already pointed out: whether or not life is full of acedia will very often depend on these little insignificant things.

The dread of doubt

Acedia, as we said, is also the temptation of doubt, the loss of certitudes. This is the devil that makes someone regret the commitment he made. After so many years spent at the monastery, apparently without any fruit, doubt insinuates itself: "What if I was mistaken?" A dreadful temptation, which threatens to topple over the whole monastery experience into non-sense. Acedia "obscure[s] the holy light in [the] eyes [of the intellect]".[18] Observances lose their

[18] Evagrius, *Antirrhētikos* VI, 16, English edition Evagrius of Pontus, *Talking Back: A Monastic Handbook for Combating Demons*, trans. David Brakke (Trappist, Ky.: Cistercian Publications; Collegeville, Minn.: Liturgical Press, 2009), 137.

significance and become inhumane. Why did I ever leave the world? Was it not, in reality, out of weakness? It would be much more useful to be in the world! Arguments like these were already found in the writings of Cassian:

> [The monk] often groans that he can do no good while he stays there [in his cell], and complains and sighs because he can bear no spiritual fruit. . . . He complains that he is cut off from spiritual gain, and is of no use in the place, as if he were one who, though he could govern others and be useful to a great number of people, yet was edifying none, nor profiting any one by his teaching and doctrine.[19]

If the monk is a priest, there is a frequent temptation to try to take on forms of ministry. "There are so many of us at the monastery, and the parishes have such a great need of priests!" A subtle but dreadful temptation, against which the Magisterium of the Church has given very clear direction:[20] if contemplative monasteries begin to take on outside ministry, they lose their distinctive vocation; it is their death.

> It would be a betrayal of the nature of the monastic institute if works were undertaken, such as the care of parishes, which would inhibit the observance proper to the monastic life, even though these works might be necessary for the pastoral life of the diocese. No matter how urgent the needs of the apostolate may be, institutes totally dedicated to contemplation cannot be called by the diocesan bishop to work in the various pastoral ministries: that would signal their ruin. However, through their spiritual witness, they

[19] John Cassian, *Institutes*, X, 2 (NPNF-2 11:267a).
[20] John Paul II, post-synodal letter *Vita Consecrata* (March 25, 1996), 8. Compare, along the same lines, the earlier *Instrumentum Laboris* for the Synod on Consecrated Life, §31, DC 2098 (1992): 682–83.

should be actively part of the diocesan family and not be isolated from it.[21]

Certainly, monasteries must serve the world; but they do not serve it in any way whatsoever.

Our life can become fruitful only in works that do not depart from the appropriate lines: the social usefulness of a contemplative is found in his contemplative life. Obviously! But it is so easy to lose sight of this! This axiom is true whether it is a question of serving his community or of serving the world.[22]

Staretz [Elder] Silouan, the holy monk of Mount Athos from the turn of the twentieth century, understood this well. It is through prayer that the monk serves the world:

Some say that monks should serve the world so as not to eat the people's bread in vain; but it must be clearly understood what this service consists of. The monk is a man who prays and weeps for the whole world; and that is his chief occupation. Who, then, incites him to weep for the whole world? The Lord Jesus Christ, the Son of God. He gives the monk the love of the Holy Spirit, and that love fills the monk's heart with sorrow for mankind, because not all of them are on the path of salvation.[23]

Through his tears and prayers he will be at the heart of the world, at the heart of the Church, in the organ that transmits life and sustains it throughout the body:

[21] *Instrumentum Laboris* for the Ninth Ordinary General Assembly of the Synod of Bishops, 1994, §78, reprinted in English as "1994 Synod/Working Paper: Consecrated Life's Role in the Church and the World", *Origins*, vol. 24, no. 7 (June 30, 1994): 97–138 at 125b.

[22] Père Jérôme, *Tout à Dieu* (Paris: Parole et Silence, 1998), 49.

[23] Silouan of Athos, cited by Archimandrite Sophrony, *Starets Silouane* (Paris: Éditions Présence, 1973), 370.

> Those who insist that contemplative Orders dedicate them-
> selves to an active apostolate, at least in part, turn them
> aside from their ultimate purpose. In the Church, contem-
> platives have the mission of being the heart, and therefore
> the most important organ, which transmits life and sustains
> it throughout the body by nourishing and strengthening it.
> God chooses persons to whom he entrusts the mission of
> praying and doing penance on behalf of their brethren in
> humanity for the glory of the Father, in pure adoration, but
> also to complete the Passion of Jesus Christ. Yes, this is the
> vocation of contemplatives, and this vocation is sublime![24]

In confronting doubt, the monk has only one path of
salvation: taking the plunge into God. Acedia insinuates
that he is useless and that he would do better to beat a
hasty retreat, to abandon the fight and leave the arena. At
the heart of that dark night, God asks him to hold on to
his hand firmly. Then, at the end of the dim corridor of
the trial, the monk will arrive at the vision of God.

The temptation of minimalism

In monastic life it may happen that everything seems to be
"too much". The Divine Office seems too long, the nights
too short, the observance of the Rule too burdensome, the
silence intolerable . . .

> At the time of the office, whenever the spirit of acedia
> should fall upon you, it suggests to the soul that psalmody
> is burdensome, and it sets laziness as an antagonist against
> the soul.[25]

---

[24] Sister Nazarena, cited by L.-A. Lassus, *Nazarena, une recluse au coeur de Rome* (Le Barroux: Éditions Sainte-Madeleine, 1996), 68–69.

[25] Evagrius, *To Eulogius* 9, in *Evagrius of Pontus: The Greek Ascetic Corpus*,

Then the temptation of minimalism appears, always supported by good reasons: "We could perfectly well be content with a little less." Then why not reduce the vigil at night? Of course, it would be so as to be able to pray better! Why not rise a little later? Certainly, that would enable us to be more orderly! Why not have a more flexible observance of the Rule? That way we would be freer to adhere to it! Why not break silence? Besides, charity should be the most important thing! . . . And so on. The list could be lengthened considerably . . .

It is striking to see how such proposals illustrate, very neatly, the dichotomy that is made in the modern world, following William of Ockham, between moral obligations for everyone and counsels pertaining only to some. We have noted this before: the morality of obligation is a morality of the minimum, and it cannot be otherwise, given the new concept of liberty introduced by modernity. If morality is reduced to the strict minimum required in order to avoid sin, then inevitably, sooner or later, those who have chosen the path of the evangelical counsels will also be tempted to reduce everything to the minimum.

Truly Christian morality, on the contrary, is a morality of total self-giving, which is proposed to all Christians, whatever their state in life. And if necessary, this self-gift can even go as far as the supreme witness of martyrdom, as John Paul II forcefully reminded us.[26] From this perspective, consecrated religious are called to manifest this total

---

trans. with introduction and commentary by Robert E. Sinkewicz (Oxford and New York: Oxford Univ. Press, 2003), 12–59 at 35.

[26] John Paul II, encyclical *Veritatis splendor* (August 6, 1993) nos. 90–93.

gift of self by an exclusive love of Christ, whom they wish to "follow . . . and imitate . . . more closely", according to the words of the Council.[27] As for contemplatives, they accomplish in prayer this total self-giving, thus manifesting the absolute priority of union with God and anticipating even now, in a way, the *gaudium* of the real union in the world to come. Even their work, far from taking them away from God, unites them to God and participates in their life of prayer.

Faced with the temptation of minimalism, the monk must rediscover the ever-new beauty of the total self-gift, renewed each day, or, rather, renewed at every moment. Above all it is necessary to recover the life of prayer and spiritual reading.

> It is necessary to pray in your cells when you are alone in the presence of God. Each of you must find—let us say—a quarter of an hour for reading, a half hour for prayer with the Psalms, if you like, or with our Jesus Prayer and other prayers. Because this paralysis sets in little by little like a sort of sleep, without causing alarm, whereas at bottom there is a great danger. The Apostle Paul, speaking to the faithful scattered throughout the Mediterranean world of his day, recommends that they fight against acedia by means of gatherings in which they can converse about the divine Word and about the things experienced by those who have gathered.[28]

The Divine Office, in particular, will be for the monk his way of renewing the total gift of himself throughout

[27] Vatican II, decree *Perfectae Caritatis*, no. 1.
[28] Archimandrite Sophrony, *Parole à la Communauté* 40 (Maldon, 2000): 1-2.

the day, throughout his life: the monk must become an "offering of praise". The Psalms, which he repeats incessantly, can always correspond to his spiritual state. Since they were prayed by Christ himself, these psalms enable the monk to have "the mind of Christ Jesus" (see Phil 2:5). Imitating Christ, he will repeat: "It is good to give thanks to the LORD!" (Ps 92:1), or else: "Into your hand I commit my spirit" (Ps 31:5).

Contemplatives witness to the primacy of the "vertical" relationship. Given a certain current of thought that tries to reduce charity to mere social service, and the Gospel to a mere message of human fraternity, the monk must remind the world that it is necessary to lift up our eyes to the heights.

> What is needed are lives that silently acclaim the primacy of God. What is needed are men who treat the Lord as Lord, who spend themselves in adoring him, who are immersed in his mystery, gratuitously and without human reward, in order to attest that he is the Absolute.[29]

Here again, the Divine Office and silent adoration are the monk's main apostolate, through which he reminds the world of the gratuitous character of time "wasted" on God, from which flows a wealth of graces for the entire Church. As someone said, "the external duty of the contemplative is to make known to others the taste for God and his light."[30]

---

[29] Conferenze Episcopale Italiana, *Messaggio del Consiglio Permanente per il XV centenario della nascita di San Benedetto* (April 15, 1980), par. 8.

[30] R. Maritain, *Journal*, in *Oeuvres complètes*, vol. 15 (Fribourg/Paris: Éditions Universitaires de Fribourg and Éditions Saint-Paul, 1995), 219.

Criticism and bitterness

Sadness, discouragement, rancor, and bitterness will certainly assume a very particular character in the setting of monastic life. Among other ways, they may manifest themselves in a certain spirit of systematic criticism that, far from strengthening community ties, only serves to cause divisions and promote a spirit of individualism. Indeed, this type of acedia is contagious: not only does one harm oneself, but one also injures others (cf. *RB* 48, 17). This is the paradox of human psychology: on the one hand, a person is himself lax and indulgent with regard to his own failings; on the other hand, he is very harsh toward his superiors and his brethren.

Someone afflicted with acedia will remember with morbid precision all the annoyances and injustices, real or imagined, that he has had to endure. Such a temptation must have been frequent in the desert, given the significant number of times Evagrius mentions it.

> Against the thought that because of listlessness [one] is moved to slander the abbot on the pretext, "He does not comfort the brothers, but he is harsh with them and does not show them mercy in their afflictions."[31]

There is no area in which man is more vulnerable than in the realm of the emotions: one feels alone, insufficiently loved, and misunderstood. Indeed, the ones responsible for this are not the brethren but, rather, one's own *ego* that is afflicted with *philautia*, that fondness of oneself that is the source of all evils.

[31] Evagrius, *Antirrhêtikos* VI, 2; *Talking Back*, 133.

By murmuring a lot and criticizing a lot, the monk forgets praise: that is when the devil of acedia does everything in his power to spoil his prayer.

> Even when he does not succeed in making him leave his cell, he [the devil of acedia] starts to distract him at the hour of the *synaxis* [liturgical assembly]: this object is not in its place, that one could very well be elsewhere. Thus he keeps him distant from divine praise and preserves his slothful, sterile spirit. All this is the fruit of inaction and carelessness.[32]

The monk then loses his spiritual respiration and runs the risk of suffocating, as though he had no more air. He will then try at all costs to "get some fresh air" outside . . . But instead of expanding his heart, in reality that will only tighten the bonds of his attachment to self, which is his real prison. He must then, on the contrary, lift up his eyes and "look toward the East" (Bar 5:5), whence will come help from the Lord; delivered from bitterness, the monk will receive the gift of peace.

> *Long-suffering is already an expression of hope.* It refuses to solve problems by any kind of attempt at break-out and escape, which does not set us free from the chains of self-absorption but often entangles us in them more deeply. No, we have to "wait upon God", look toward him patiently and faithfully in prayer. Such waiting amid the dark trials of *acedia* is like walking in thick fog. Everything seems blurred, with no way forward and no way out. But then suddenly the fog begins to break. The sun burns it away, and brilliant daylight shines forth. So it is with the temptation of *acedia*.

[32] Antiochus de Saint-Sabas, *Homélie* 26; French trans. É. Goutagny, in *La voie royale du désert: Apophtegmes* (Désiris, 1996), 205.

Suddenly it disappears, and one is left with deep peace and unutterable joy. Hope has triumphed.[33]

The monk has left everything to follow Christ (cf. Mt 19:27). In reality, although "following Jesus" and "leaving everything" go hand in hand, it is necessary *first of all* to follow Christ in order to be able to leave everything. Indeed, only to the extent that I follow him, that I walk in his footsteps so as to become his disciple little by little, do I discover how cluttered my life is, how much I need to be set free. At the beginning of monastic life, we are ready to make radical sacrifices. We would like to leave everything, give everything. But, very quickly, we discover that God always asks of us something that we had not thought of, sometimes even apparently insignificant things of which we are incapable of letting go.

To follow Jesus, therefore, is to embark on a veritable discovery of oneself, a discovery of all those secret attachments, those unconfessed refusals, those secret wounds. We would have liked to leave everything, we were aspiring to freedom, and here we discover, with a sort of disillusionment that can sometimes lead to despair or turn into cynicism, that we are caught in our own trap. And if we are somewhat lucid and honest with ourselves, we can dare to acknowledge that following Jesus, leaving everything for him, is beyond our capacity. We then realize that, despite all our efforts and our good resolutions, in fact we have not yet really begun!

---

[33] Christoph Schönborn, *Loving the Church: Retreat to John Paul II and the Papal Household* (San Francisco: Ignatius Press, 1998), 162.

But, paradoxically, this realization of our resistance, of our inability to respond to his call, is perhaps, in reality, the most precious fruit, the most beautiful thing about the monastic experience. For when we have consented to our own poverty, then God can finally begin to work within us. When everything seems obstructed, then the emergency exit appears; when we can do no more, then God can finally begin his work!

To conclude we will use once again the metaphor of the abode. The monk's whole battle consists of attaining the freedom to dwell in peace in his own heart so as to abide in God. The greatest thing that Pope Saint Gregory said in praise of Saint Benedict is no doubt found in this expression: "He lived alone with himself" (*habitavit secum*),[34] in other words, he had unified his life and directed all his energies toward God alone. The monk is called to live in his intimate depths and, from there, to take charge of the conduct of his life.

Acedia appears, in the case of a monk, precisely as the temptation to stop "dwelling alone with himself", in other words, to stop orienting his whole life toward God. We see, therefore, how it is a threat to monastic activity itself. Today it is again necessary to rediscover the fundamental insights of the "athletes of the desert". They understood that the spiritual combat against thoughts, and against acedia in particular, leads to purity of heart: the monk's action then becomes action guided by the Spirit. Only from this point of departure can the monk discover the place

[34] Gregory the Great, *Dialogues* II, 3, 5; FOC 39:62–63.

that is assigned to him in the world and in the Church and accomplish what he is called to do. Delivered from acedia, he will then become for everyone, near and far, a peacemaker.

Acedia in Priestly Life

In 2006, then-Cardinal Jorge Mario Bergoglio preached an Ignatian retreat to the bishops of Spain. He devoted one short conference to acedia in the life of pastors. Here is an excerpt:

> Acedia can take on various guises in our life as pastors, so we need to remain alert in order to discern how it camouflages itself. At times it appears as paralysis, when one can no longer accept the rhythm of life. At other times, it is the hyperactive pastor whose giddy comings and goings reveal an inability to ground himself in God and in his concrete circumstances. On other occasions, acedia manifests itself in ambitious plans hatched without any attention to the nitty gritty involved in getting such a project off the ground, let alone sustaining it. Conversely, it can take the form of getting tied up in knots about immediate details, unable to integrate them within the larger vision of God's plan. In this context, the epitaph of Saint Ignatius is instructive: "Not to be confined by the greatest, yet to be contained within the smallest, is divine" (*Non coerceri a maximo, sed contineri a minimo divinum est*). It is important to recognize that acedia is a divisive and debilitating force; what unites is life, and those under the sway of acedia are deprived of life.[35]

[35] Jorge Mario Bergoglio (Pope Francis), *In Him Alone Is Our Hope: The Church according to the Heart of Pope Francis* (New York, Paris, Madrid, and Oxford: Magnificat, 2013), 57–58.

Acedia therefore does affect the pastors of the Church. With regard to priestly life, I will speak more briefly, however, and will simply suggest a few of the specific characteristics of acedia in the life of the priest.

Discouragement

This is no doubt the most obvious manifestation of acedia today among priests, even among the younger clergy. We will never make it; it is too difficult! Given the continually decreasing number of priests, the individual collapses under the weight of the responsibility. Moreover, the external results are truly meager: after so much trouble and effort, the small number of faithful at Mass has scarcely increased, the young people are no longer going to church, fewer and fewer Catholics are receiving the sacraments, and so on.

After the first months or the first few years spent in giving without counting the cost, and sometimes even without measure, one may experience the "collapse of the soul" of which Evagrius spoke, a collapse that has physiological and psychological repercussions, since acedia is found precisely at the limit of one's bodily and spiritual capacities. The priest is then prey to the deepest discouragement, which can even lead him to question his vocation: "What if I was mistaken?" But is this not fundamentally a lack of faith? It can happen when the priest no longer has a sufficiently supernatural outlook to be able to see things as God sees them. God did not promise us success here on earth. He himself willed to save the world, not in a magnificent public victory, but, on the contrary, through the ignominy and utter solitude of a death that in human terms was absurd. "Unless a grain of wheat falls into the earth and dies" (Jn 12:24).

> First of all, . . . one certainty: God does not fail. He "fails" continuously, but for this very reason he does not fail, because through this he finds new opportunities for far greater mercy and his imagination is inexhaustible. He does not fail because he finds ever new ways to reach people and to open wider his great house so that it is completely filled.[36]

When one no longer has faith in oneself, when one no longer has faith in the Church, then one no longer has sufficient strength to guide the flock. How could the captain of a ship set out in a vessel he thinks is leaking? Now, the Church is not a leaking boat, because the Lord promises his help until the end of time (Mt 28:20). Confronted with the apparent failure of his ministry, the priest is called to remember that he sowed or watered, but God is the one who gives the growth (1 Cor 3:6). What the Lord asks is the gift of self, more than apostolic activities; the gift of self, in the image of Christ's gift to his Church:

> The essential content of this pastoral charity is the *gift of self*, the total gift of self *to the Church*, following the example of Christ. Pastoral charity is the virtue by which we imitate Christ in his self-giving and service. It is not just what we do, but our gift of self, which manifests Christ's love for his flock. Pastoral charity determines our way of thinking and acting, our way of relating to people.[37]

---

[36] Benedict XVI, homily, Mass with members of the Bishops' Conference of Switzerland (November 7, 2006).

[37] John Paul II, post-synodal apostolic exhortation *Pastores dabo vobis* (1992), no. 23.

A prophetic sign

The priest's life is and, furthermore, will always be in-comprehensible from the human perspective: God alone explains its meaning. It is so mysterious that the priest must give up trying to "understand himself"; he has only to keep his eyes fixed unceasingly on God.

> And it is only through God in Christ that we receive the guarantee that whoever leaves everything "for my sake and for the sake of the gospel" does not fall into the void, does not fall between two stools, but (as he hangs) will be borne along in his impossible existence. That such a person can have no sort of "self-understanding" must be clear; he has given up interpreting himself, so that he may be interpreted by God alone. He does not judge himself but holds himself open to God's direction, who knows him and judges him aright. It is the fact that he has abandoned his self-understanding that makes him the priest I want, one who with his existence can become for me a word and a light of God.[38]

In fact, only on this condition will he be able to trans-mit to others a light that does not come from himself, the fire of Divine Love. The priest therefore must not seek the meaning of his life in worldly effectiveness: otherwise, ace-dia would be precisely this temptation to conform to the present world. The priest would fall into activism, which, as Evagrius and Cassian noted, is another subtle form of ace-dia: indeed, it is the temptation to erase the supernatural as-pect of action, so as to keep only the aspect of profitability.

[38] Hans Urs von Balthasar, "The Priest that I Want", in *Elucidations* (San Francisco: Ignatius Press, 1998), 161–72 at 166–67.

Then the priest becomes nothing more than a "functionary of God", whereas he ought to be the witness to the gratuitousness of the gift: the priesthood takes up all of a man's time, because it takes the whole man.

> The abandonment of existence with its own light is the thing that alone provides the guarantee of the essential humility which makes a man transparent for a life other than his own, which shines forth with a light which does not interest the man who has abandoned himself, on which he does not reflect, which he does not cultivate. The fire which burns in the truly humble man is that of love for God and for his incarnate word; it does not have its focus in the man himself but in the object of his love.[39]

The priest must continue to be a prophetic sign, just like the consecrated religious. Now a prophet is someone who disturbs the complacent. He disturbs because he is a constant call to radical conversion. A prophet denounces sloth and invites others to give up merely human means of security, so as to allow themselves to be guided by God himself. The prophet's preaching is not a human project but the initiative of the Holy Spirit: the prophet is the one who lives under the continual influence of the Spirit, because he is always willing to let himself be guided and moved by the Spirit. Only if he allows himself to be guided by the Spirit will the priest's apostolic activity be effective (even if there is no visible result), for it will be action "in the Spirit".

The priest is called to holiness in a very special way. But there is no reason to think of this holiness as something

[39] Ibid., 167.

independent of his ministry. On the contrary, it is precisely
in his ministry that he will be sanctified.

> Therefore, an intimate bond exists between the priest's
> spiritual life and the exercise of his ministry, a bond which
> the Council expresses in this fashion: "And so it is that they
> are grounded in the life of the Spirit while they exercise
> the ministry of the Spirit and of justice (cf. 2 Cor. 3:8–
> 9), as long as they [priests] are docile to Christ's Spirit,
> who gives them life and guidance. For by their everyday
> sacred actions, as by the entire ministry which they exer-
> cise in union with the bishop and their fellow priests, they
> are being directed toward perfection of life. Priestly holi-
> ness itself contributes very greatly to a fruitful fulfillment
> of the priestly ministry" [*Presbyterorum Ordinis* 12].[40]

This is why the priest must go so far as to sacrifice his
life for his mission. This total gift of his person is what
makes a good priest, and this is always a miracle of grace.

> A good priest is always a miracle of grace. . . . The mira-
> cle for which one is looking would indeed be nothing other
> than sanctity: sanctity of a man who in God has become so
> unimportant to himself that for him only God still counts.
> Who he himself is, is no longer a matter of any concern to
> him. And in consequence he is as ordinary and as nourish-
> ing as a loaf of bread from which everyone can break off a
> piece. The manner in which he distributes himself merges
> into the manner in which God's word distributes itself in
> bread and wine. Such a man knows too how one breaks
> and expounds God's word.[41]

---

[40] John Paul II, *Pastores Dabo Vobis*, 24.
[41] Von Balthasar, "The Priest that I Want", 168, 170.

This priestly grace, which is capable of miracles, requires, nevertheless, an open, docile heart; otherwise, acedia will reappear in force.

Activism and compensations

The activism of priests is often the counterpart of a lack of prayer. When time is short, something has to give. There is indeed a great danger that what is sacrificed will be one's prayer life. Abandoned at first for what the priest thinks are pastoral "necessities", prayer can eventually become impossible and even intolerable. Then it is truly acedia in the full sense: disgust with one's relationship with God. But since the spiritual life of the priest is intimately bound up with his priestly activity, the abandonment of the life of prayer causes a veritable "disgust with priestly activity", in other words, with the activity belonging specifically to the priest.

The priest no longer has time to pray, but paradoxically he happens to "waste time" in secondary or even plainly harmful activities. I am thinking, in particular, of the sensitive question of using the internet and social networks. Although the new means of communication are a valuable aid for practical ministry and personal formation and are obviously an organizational time-saver, we must not forget the dangers they pose for the spiritual life: the loss of time, superficial relationships, real dangers to purity of heart and of the body, loss of freedom, and dulling of the conscience. How many priests admit having trouble managing their relationship with the internet, recognizing that they devote too much time to it, with the risk of making it an opportunity to compensate for the difficulties inherent in the performance of their daily ministry!

Prayer, the sacraments, and reading the Word of God are absolutely necessary for a priest: indeed, the Word itself is his "abode". How could he continue to offer spiritual nourishment if he no longer nourishes himself? How could he be the minister of God's forgiveness if he no longer experiences it for himself?

> The priest's celebration of the Eucharist and administration of the other sacraments, his pastoral zeal, his relationship with the faithful, his communion with his brother priests, his collaboration with his bishop, his life of prayer—in a word, the whole of his priestly existence, suffers an inexorable decline if by negligence or for some other reason he fails to receive the sacrament of penance at regular intervals and in a spirit of genuine faith and devotion. If a priest were no longer to go to confession or properly confess his sins, his priestly being and his priestly action would feel its effects very soon, and this would also be noticed by the community of which he was the pastor.[42]

Clearly, priestly identity and also *priestly action* are at stake here. Therefore, whether as neglect of prayer or distaste for it, acedia threatens, in the case of the priest as well, to affect the activity that belongs specifically to him, *priestly* action, by causing it to lose its sanctifying dimension.

The ecclesial communion

Another manifestation of acedia, in the life of the priest, may be the temptation to "choose" his ministry himself

---

[42] John Paul II, *Pastores Dabo Vobis*, 26, citing *Reconciliatio paenitentia*, 31.

instead of "receiving" it from the Church. Moreover, this can be done very subtly. The priest "feels" called to this or that mission, for which he has a preference or the qualifications. He thinks that he has some particular charism. Now certainly, the Lord asks us, in the Gospel, to invest our talents and not to bury them (cf. Mt 25:18). But that does not mean that our personal flourishing or the fulfillment of our desires is the norm for our action or the criterion for our ministry.

This may give rise to a bitter attitude toward authority, when it seems to "go against" our own initiatives. We must never forget that our ministry should be "received" and that we do not give it to ourselves. Faithfulness in the austerity of the daily routine, perseverance in the ministry that has been received, on the contrary, are a good criterion for the authenticity and fruitfulness of this ministry. Now the identity of the priest is revealed in depth within the Church, understood as mystery of trinitarian communion: therefore, only by immersing himself in this mystery will the priest be able to fight against acedia, which is a sin against communion.

> [T]he nature and mission of the ministerial priesthood cannot be defined except through this multiple and rich interconnection of relationships which arise from the Blessed Trinity and are prolonged in the communion of the Church, as a sign and instrument of Christ, of communion with God and of the unity of all humanity. In this context the ecclesiology of communion becomes decisive for understanding the identity of the priest, his essential dignity, and his vocation and mission among the People of God and in the world.[43]

---

[43] Ibid., 12.

In the life of a priest, acedia can therefore manifest itself in weariness or discouragement with his ministry, but also, more radically, in an excessive conformity to the world or a loss of priestly identity. Just as in the case of monastic life, acedia threatens therefore to affect the dynamism of priestly activity. Only in humility can the priest remain faithful: understanding that he is not up to his ministry, he will have to let the Spirit take possession of him more and more each day, and of his emotional and spiritual dynamics as well. Only in this way will he be able to attain sanctity, a holiness that is given to him yet is also the fruit of his fidelity.

> Holiness consists of such a state of poverty that at every moment one is obliged to ask everything of the Holy Spirit, one is dependent on him, awaiting his help, convinced that without his grace one can do nothing. This is the formation that God imposes on the souls with which he wills to work. He infuses docility in them through poverty; he turns them into beggars so as to make them docile.[44]

Only Christ is truly Priest: a man who is called to become a priest merely participates in the priesthood of Christ. Therefore only by radically conforming himself to Christ's priestly action—a conformity that is still the work of the Spirit—will the priest be able to make present the invaluable treasure of the Good Shepherd's Love.

---

[44] Marie-Eugène de l'Enfant-Jésus, cited by R. Règue, *Viens Esprit Saint* (Venasque: Éditions du Carmel, 1998), 280.

Acedia: Sin against the Spiritual Fruitfulness of a Married Couple

Now we have arrived at the last state of life that we want to consider: marriage. Can we actually speak about acedia in marriage? In the case of monastic life, certainly; in the case of priestly life it applies, too; but for a married couple? Is not acedia the concern of hermits? No, unfortunately: what we have said already indicates it plainly enough. It affects every individual, even though it may be by the most roundabout paths.

> Is not acedia said to be the temptation of the recluse? For the ancients, it is clear that it was not reserved for anchorites alone or even for cenobites. The spiritual combat is not enclosed within a "stadium" apart from ordinary life. If Christ went to the desert to confront the Prince of this world, in that face-to-face encounter which the Gospels record for us, it is because nowhere else does the latter manifest himself so clearly; but it was also in order to begin the combat that he would then wage day after day in the midst of men and even unto the cross. . . . The difference between the desert and the world is that in one, the tempter attacks recluses "with his bare hands", through thoughts, whereas in the other, he uses intermediaries, which are things, people, and pressures to conform. . . . The passions are the same everywhere. In society they are just veiled by the agitation of the world.[45]

At the origin of marital love: an act of faith

We can say that every life begins with an act of faith that engenders it and then guides it in its development. Marital

---

[45] C. Flipo, "L'acédie dans la tradition spirituelle", *Christus* 157 (1993): 59.

love commits the spouses to a new life and makes them givers of life. How could a man and a woman form a life-long covenant without a very personal act of faith at the beginning of their union? This faith involves a knowledge of the other that is altogether different from scientific knowledge: it is an intimate, all-encompassing, intuitive knowledge. This is the knowledge belonging to love, affective knowledge that functions by a sort of connaturality with the beloved. This knowledge is found at the very heart of love and helps it to grow thanks to fidelity, which is the essential quality of faith.

This is precisely the image of this *conjugal faith* that Scripture uses when it tries to present the covenant between God and his people, the union between Christ and the Church and, through her, with every believer. We saw earlier the connections that join faith and acedia, even though the latter is ultimately a sin against charity. Acedia manifests itself above all as a temptation to infidelity and a lack of trust, which urge a spouse to leave the marital communion.

Leaving the marital communion

Saint Thomas described acedia as the sin against the *gaudium* that results from union with the Beloved. He defined it also as disgust with working, with that action which was aimed specifically at a communion of persons. I insisted on the fact that acedia, as disgust that paralyzes action, was a sin against communion, a sin opposed to the gift of self. It therefore causes the subject to turn in on himself, instead of making him enter into the logic of the gift. Although that was true about ecclesial communion, as we showed in the preceding chapter, it can be observed very especially in marital communion, in which the two spouses have given themselves totally to each other in the sacrament of marriage, in the image of the gift of Christ to his Bride, the Church.

> In order to understand better the foundations, the contents and the characteristics of this participation [of the family in the Church], we must examine the many profound bonds linking the Church and the Christian family and establishing the family as a "Church in miniature" (*Ecclesia domestica*), in such a way that in its own way the family is a living image and historical representation of the mystery of the Church.[46]

For this logic of the gift is indeed at the heart of the conjugal mystery. In fact, the *communio personarum* finds its perfection in the mystery of God, One and Triune: the Father gives himself totally to his Son without keeping anything for himself; he engenders him. The Son returns everything to the Father; he gives himself back to the Father. This exchange of love between the two Divine Persons is such that it is infinitely fruitful: it gives rise to another Person, the Holy Spirit, the Gift par excellence. Now man is made in the image of God, not only in his ability to understand and to will, but also in his ability to enter into communion. So it is that we can say that the communion of persons between a man and a woman actualizes, for the human person, the fact of being the image of God.

Although acedia is a sin against the communion of the Christian with his God, it is also a sin against the communion of Christians with each other. In the specific context

---

[46] John Paul II, post-synodal apostolic exhortation *Familiaris consortio* (November 22, 1981), no. 49.

of the married couple, acedia will appear as the danger of leaving the marital communion, that "abode of action" belonging to the spouses. Pope John Paul I could say humorously, during his first Wednesday audience, that marriage sometimes appeared like a cage, from which the couple wanted to get out!

> Once I wrote an article in the newspaper in which I took the liberty of making a joke by citing Montaigne, a French writer, who said: "Marriage is like a cage: those who are outside do everything they can to get in, while those who are inside do all they can to get out." But several days later I received a letter from a retired education official, who had written books, and he reproached me, saying: "Your Excellency, you were wrong to cite Montaigne; my wife and I have been married for sixty years and every day is like the first." And then he cited for me a French poet, in French, but I cite it in Italian: "Every day I love you more, today much more than yesterday, but much less than tomorrow." That is what I wish for you![47]

Indeed, true love is ever new. Therefore it is within their marital communion that spouses must learn, in their imitation of Christ, to realize their full potential in the radical gift of themselves: this is the "locus" of their mutual self-donation.

> The only "place" in which this self-giving in its whole truth is made possible is marriage, the covenant of conjugal love freely and consciously chosen, whereby man and woman accept the intimate community of life and love willed by God Himself which only in this light manifests its true meaning.[48]

---

[47] John Paul I, General Audience, September 6, 1978.
[48] John Paul II, *Familiaris consortio*, no. 11.

Although fidelity is a battle, Christ nevertheless promises victory to the one who has agreed to give himself totally: "Whoever would save his life will lose it; and whoever loses his life for my sake and the gospel's will save it" (Mk 8:35).

Lack of openness to children

Acedia can manifest itself as the withdrawal of each spouse into himself. But it can also affect the spouses as a couple and manifest itself through a lack of openness to the children that God may give them. Here we come to the important affirmation of the inseparability of the two dimensions of marital love: union and procreation. Indeed, marital life is not merely a union of persons: it is a union of persons capable of procreation. Only to the extent that the spouses are open to receiving a new life, the fruit of their love, is their union truly a marital union.

> Mutual betrothed love demands a union of persons. But the union of persons is not the same as sexual union. This latter is raised to the level of the person only when it is accompanied in the mind and the will by acceptance of the possibility of parenthood. This acceptance is so important, so decisive that without it marital intercourse cannot be said to be a realization of the personal order.[49]

If the potential for paternity and maternity are excluded from marital relations, radically and totally, then by that very fact the mutual relationship of the persons is transformed, and it loses its truly "personal" character. Ace-

---

[49] Karol Wojtyła, *Love and Responsibility*, trans. H. T. Willetts (London: William Collins Sons & Co., and New York: Farrar, Straus and Giroux, 1981; reprinted San Francisco: Ignatius Press, 1993), 228.

dia can manifest itself also by a selfish withdrawal of the couple into itself, in the rejection of the natural fecundity of their love. Acedia then falsifies the language of their bodies, through which communion is achieved. In order to elaborate such an argument, it is necessary to go back to the ultimate significance of love, within the Trinity.

> [The] power and nobility [of the marital act] come of the unique communion it brings about; so intimate that it absorbs the whole person in all his mystery: wherefore it is one of the gravest acts open to man and woman. Its tragic possibilities are due to the fact that communion is here realized by means of the body. If the union of man and woman is the fruit of a love that is given in purity, generosity and fidelity, then the body itself is spiritualized in the service of a love that ennobles it, and, with God's blessing, sanctifies. Then man remains man, that is to say a flesh sustained by a spirit. If the union is the issue of an instinct devoid of generosity, of a gift made without purity, of an attraction involving no fidelity, then the soul itself is abased, degraded, gradually reduced to the same level of carnality and animality as the love that drags it down: and the man, thus fallen beneath himself, now becomes no more than a spirit miserably fettered to the senses.[50]

Man is the image of God not only as a person but also inasmuch as he is capable of interpersonal communion: human love, in its true form, is communion between two persons of the opposite sex that is open to a third person. The gift of the sacrament is the fact that the love of the spouses shares in the trinitarian love: there is an "existential analogy between the Gift of God to the spouses and the

[50] Jean Mouroux, *The Meaning of Man* (New York: Sheed & Ward, 1948), 56.

gift of the spouses to God".[51] In this context, we redis-cover the perspective, which by now has become generally accepted in ecclesial doctrine, on the child as "the most excellent gift of marriage", which reiterates in depth the mystery of procreation in the language of the gift. Acedia can thus be considered the self-encapsulation of the cou-ple, a closure that darkens their hearts and prevents them from thinking about love in terms of gift.

> In the conjugal act, husband and wife are called to confirm in a responsible way *the mutual gift* of self which they have made to each other in the marriage covenant. The logic of the *total gift of self to the other* involves a potential openness to procreation: in this way the marriage is called to even greater fulfilment as a family. . . . *The intimate truth of this gift* must always be *safeguarded.*[52]

Rejecting the mystery of life

We showed earlier that acedia was the noonday devil, the devil of an excess of light, that leads one to deny the mys-tery. A society affected by acedia ends up affirming that the sciences must be able to explain everything, prove ev-erything; moreover, it thinks that it is legitimate—or even necessary—to implement and experience all that science is capable of achieving. We see the tragic relevance today of such an ideology, particularly in questions of bioethics. But this is true also in the realm of spousal love, this "great mystery" of which Saint Paul speaks (Eph 5:32).

[51] See M. Ouellet, "Pour une théologie des 'dons' du mariage", *Anthropotes* 13 (1997): 495–503 at 499.
[52] John Paul II, *Letter to Families* (1994), 12.

Modern rationalism *does not tolerate mystery*. It does not accept the mystery of man as male and female, nor is it willing to admit that the full truth about man has been revealed in Jesus Christ. In particular, it does not accept the "great mystery" proclaimed in the Letter to the Ephesians, but radically opposes it. It may well acknowledge, in the context of a vague deism, the possibility and even the need for a supreme or divine Being, but it firmly rejects the idea of a God who became man in order to save man. For rationalism it is unthinkable that God should be the Redeemer, much less *that he should be "the Bridegroom"*, the primordial and unique source of the human love between spouses. . . . The deep-seated roots of the "great mystery", the sacrament of love and life which began with Creation and Redemption and which *has Christ the Bridegroom as its ultimate surety*, have been lost in the modern way of looking at things. The "great mystery" is threatened in us and all around us.[53]

Do we not see an example of this rejection of mystery, in marital life, in the mad efforts of science to produce— or worse, to "manufacture"—new human beings in the laboratory? In this desire to get a child at any cost, or in the desire to choose his qualities and characteristics in advance, is there not a lack of respect for the mystery of life, which God asks us, instead, to welcome and receive as a gift? Parents are called pro-creators, in other words, sharers in God's creative act. They alone are not the creators of their child. They receive him as the most marvelous gift they could ever obtain. The true light is not science, but rather a light that has no frightening excess: Christ himself.

[53] Ibid., 19.

"I have come as light into the world, that whoever believes in me may not remain in darkness" (Jn 12:46).

Compensations outside the family

If the first symptom of acedia, according to the Desert Fathers, was the temptation to leave one's cell because it seemed too confining, it seems that nowadays the marital abode can also be regarded as too narrow! How can anyone take the risk of committing himself forever to sharing life with just one spouse who, in the final analysis, is still fragile and limited and may change over time? Moreover, as we said, acedia is that paralysis of action which originates with regard to friendship with God and with neighbor.

From these two manifestations it is clear that "fleeing one's cell" can also mean losing the dynamism of "marital" action, in other words, the action belonging specifically to spouses, the action in which they encounter God and anticipate, by the intimate communion as husband and wife, the total communion with God in the beatific vision. The spouse afflicted with acedia who succumbs to the temptation of flight finds himself deprived of the impetus that drove him to act for the good of the conjugal communion.

Then there is a risk that he will start looking for compensations outside the nuclear family. These may be affections, or else secondary liaisons, work, sports, various activities . . . Moreover some very good pretexts will be offered to justify these compensations. Evagrius had already pointed them out: visiting the sick, performing one's family duties, or better serving the living God. It can happen, for example, that external commitments made by a father or a mother of a family, even in the parish community, may be in reality a flight from the duties of their state and from everyday life at home. Indeed, in married life it is quite possible for routine to set in and to become intolerable one day, because of the loss of the interior dynamism that results from the ceaselessly renewed gift of self.

We spoke about the importance of rediscovering forgiveness, both given and received, as an excellent act that participates in the gratuitous action of Christ, an action that assumed the form of an unlimited pardon given to his Bride, the Church, a pardon that has extraordinary fruitfulness. The action of Christian spouses will thus become the place of their communion with Christ, the source of the communion between them. Of course, forgiveness costs something: the effort must ceaselessly be made anew, so as to have the interior availability needed to give and also to receive forgiveness. But ultimately it is the source of peace and joy.[54] Furthermore, in the case where one of the spouses has gone away, forgiveness enables him to come back home, where the other must be ready with open arms to welcome him once again. "It was fitting to make merry and be glad, for this your brother was dead, and is alive; he was lost, and is found" (Lk 15:32). Having returned to the marital abode, the Christian spouse is once again fully reintegrated into the community of the children of God, thereby sharing in the circulation of the sap of life and bearing fruit for the salvation of the world (Jn 15:5).[55]

[54] The reader may consult: V. Siret, "La place libre, signe du pardon toujours offert", *Anthropotes* 11 (1995): 183–200.

[55] Concerning forgiveness between spouses, the reader may consult: J. Laffitte, *Le Pardon transfiguré* (Paray-le-Monial: Éditions de l'Emmanuel, 1996).

The perpetual search for novelty

Another area where the perpetual search for novelty may appear is the area of the couple's sexual life. It can happen that this becomes a mere personal quest for maximum pleasure or for new sensations, a sort of "sexual babbling".

> The worst pitfall for sexuality that is considered to be not that important is insignificance. The easier a thing is, the greater the risk that it will lose its value by losing its price. The gestures of sexuality will have value and meaning only if they are the result of a whole gradual approach, a crossing of a distance, a victory over obstacles; if each of the partners has the sense that something important is at stake. Without that, it remains at the level of sexual babbling, in which even the most intimate gestures end up losing their savor.[56]

Now the sexual life of a couple should be, on the contrary, the deepening of an encounter between two persons, a meeting that will be ever new inasmuch as it is a question of making the other more and more happy, and not of seeking one's own pleasure. Acedia could then be a sin against the couple's chastity, inasmuch as desire is not integrated with love but is sought for its own sake. However, it would soon be disappointing:

> The danger is that it [desire] may become an end in itself, the first and foremost goal in life. That has two disadvantages: on the one hand, it can be an obstacle to the search for greater goods; on the other hand, the person of the other spouse is then liable to become a means. Finally, it turns out that the more a desire is sought for its own sake, the more ambiguous and disappointing it will be. Its true

[56] X. Lacroix, "Le corps et l'esprit", *Vie chrétienne* (1996): 28.

nature is to be neither an end nor a means, but a sign, a gift.
The sign of some good, a gift along the path of the quest
for it: thanksgiving, encounter, revelation of the other to
oneself and of oneself to the other.[57]

Given the frenzy for novelty, the couple is called to return again and again to the Word of God, which calls the
spouses every day and is always new: "Morning by morning he wakens, he wakens my ear to hear as those who
are taught" (Is 50:4). The spouses are called to discover
each day the revelation of love that is ever new. For there
is indeed one kind of repetition that should be rejected:
that is the sterile repetition of something that is "always
the same"; on the contrary, it is a question of welcoming
one's spouse anew, each day, so as to allow him or her
to grow.

In order to understand correctly the true sense of marital fecundity, it is necessary to go back to the mystery of
Christ and the Church and, even farther, to the mystery of
the ever-new fecundity that springs up within the life of
the Trinity and then pours out on the couple created in its
image. To do that we would have to reread the profound
passages by Adrienne von Speyr or Hans Urs von Balthasar
on the spiritual fecundity of the married couple in light of
the mystery of Christ's union with the Church and in light
of the figure of Mary.

Acedia, therefore, can be considered the sin against
the spiritual fecundity of the married couple. In this
sense, it, too, affects the dynamism of the action proper to
spouses, the dynamism of marital action. Being a sin against

[57] Ibid., 35.

communion, it makes spouses forget that the human person is fulfilled only in the unreserved gift of self and that the mutual belonging of spouses is a sign of the relation of Christ to his Church. Whereas spouses are called to become "a saving community",[58] acedia in contrast makes them self-contained and causes them to think that fidelity is impossible. However, as with the other states of life, by their perseverance (*hypomonē*)[59] in staying in their own "abode", Christian spouses will contribute to the building up of the Body of Christ. United spiritually, in an altogether special way, to those who are called to virginity for the sake of the Kingdom, they should know that, thanks to their prayer and to the offering of themselves, they will unite themselves to the fruitful Vine that is Christ, thus bearing fruit for the Church and for the world.

> Thus the Christian family's actual participation in the Church's life and mission is in direct proportion to the fidelity and intensity of the prayer with which it is united with the fruitful vine that is Christ the Lord. The fruitfulness of the Christian family in its specific service to human advancement, which of itself cannot but lead to the transformation of the world, derives from its living union with Christ, nourished by Liturgy, by self-oblation and by prayer.[60]

What about single persons?

There is such a thing as celibacy consecrated to God: it is the celibacy of religious men and women, of priests,

---

[58] John Paul II, *Familiaris consortio*, no. 49.

[59] Since *hypomonē* means, literally, the act of "remaining under the yoke", this virtue certainly plays an altogether essential role in the life of "wedded partners", those who are "yokefellows".

[60] John Paul II, *Familiaris consortio*, no. 62.

and of some lay people, also. But being single, per se, is a much more widespread state of life, lived out incidentally in widely divergent ways. Often being single is like a lot of other things in life: one finds oneself thrown into the situation without having chosen it. Without a destination, without a plan. But man, who is endowed with an intellect, can give meaning to it. For although being single is similar to "waiting"—waiting for a spouse, for an ecclesial commitment, for a good reason to live—it is possible to find within this state a call, a vocation, a meaning that, this time, can be chosen.

However, this sort of being single is often experienced as "poverty" in comparison with what appears to be "wealth", in other words, married life, children, and so on. Poverty signifies a lack, and a lasting one, for we are not talking here about the temporary state of being single in youth. Does this lack mean the failure of one's whole life, a form of suffering for which there is no compensation? A desert, an irremediable absence of fruitfulness? It is obvious how the devil of acedia threatens to affect single persons, also. Within the restricted context here, let us point out three avenues of reflection that would need to be explored at greater length.

First of all, it is important not to rush into a facile optimism that denies the difficulties of being single. It is necessary to acknowledge clearly the existence of single people, who are constantly at risk of being forgotten in favor of married people and those who have been called to consecrated celibacy—even though the latter also experience trials of their own. Think of their loneliness on holidays or Sundays, when single people find themselves alone upon leaving Mass, whereas the others are going to spend the day with their family; think of the loneliness in the evenings when, once the day is done, they go back home to find . . . four walls! Think of the loneliness of heart, even in the midst of friends, which is often made even more bitter at the sight of those who are not alone. Here, acedia can manifest itself as the feeling of being excluded, outsiders to society or even to the Church. However, the Church must show solicitude toward all. We can reread, for this purpose, this short passage recalling the solicitude of pastors of the Church toward single persons.

> We must also remember the great number of *single persons* who, because of the particular circumstances in which they have to live—often not of their choosing—are especially close to Jesus' heart and therefore deserve the special affection and active solicitude of the Church, especially of pastors. Many remain *without a human family*. . . . The doors of homes, the "domestic churches," and of the great family which is the Church must be open to all of them. "No one is without a family in this world: the Church is a home and family for everyone, especially those who 'labor and are heavy laden.'"[61]

Next, we must recognize the situation of single persons, without minimizing the difficulties and sufferings, but also without overlooking the joys and opportunities. For although emotional solitude or even sexual frustration may be sensed painfully by single persons, especially if their professional life offers them little recognition or gratification, it is nevertheless true that neither a spouse nor a child nor a job is what gives profound meaning to life. Rather, it

[61] CCC 1658, citing *Familiaris consortio*, no. 85, and Mt 11:28.

is the capacity for love and for the freedom that one can lay down and take up again at every moment, a capacity that finds its source in the personal relationship of the single person with Christ.

> Above all it is about finding in oneself the thing that is the source of joy and life and then making it burst forth outside. Undeniably, this will be easier for the single person who finds his source of life in Jesus Christ. In his personal relationship with the Lord, maintained in prayer and the regular reception of the sacraments, he will learn to love and esteem himself, regardless of the views of others, to invest his exchanges with more authenticity, to recollect himself and remain in interior peace.[62]

Everything makes sense then! Beginning with the everyday things that the devil of acedia might have belittled as trite and routine. Each single person possesses qualities, gifts, and even charisms that he can and must place at the service of all. Each single person has abilities to love that he can awaken in friendship also.

Finally, as a matter of principle we must be convinced that everyone can take part in the gospel and in the mission of the Church. Thus, the single life, even when not chosen, is a call to go beyond oneself. It is an invitation to love with a disinterested, universal love. But this necessarily occurs by way of accepting one's poverty. Over the years, the single person must resign himself to the loss of the spouse and the parent that he would have liked to be and that he would no doubt have been quite capable of being. Then that poverty, accepted and offered up in prayer, will

[62] C. Lesegrétain, "Rester célibataire . . . sans l'avoir 'choisi'", *Christus*, 226 HS (2010): 129–35 at 133.

become the source of great graces for the Church and the world.

> All celibacy lived out with trust in God and in fidelity to Christ yields spiritual graces. Beginning with a grace of *intercession* . . . , especially for those who suffer from isolation and loneliness. Another grace given to all who acknowledge that they are poor is the grace of *love for the Church*. Single persons who are not consecrated religious are fully members of the People of God, but they are also particularly close to the heart of Jesus. . . . A third spiritual grace yielded by celibacy lived out in fidelity to Christ is the grace of *fruitfulness*. This fruitfulness is not measured by the number of children or accomplishments; it depends neither on talents nor efforts, but corresponds to an interior availability and faithfulness to God.[63]

Thus the single person will combat the third possible manifestation of acedia in his life, namely, thinking that his life is sterile and unproductive. We are all called to bear fruit, to be productive. In a society where people seek to be protected and fulfilled, single persons can be signposts recalling that only the God of Love can satisfy the thirst of the human heart. And although acedia incites us to flee into the past or the future, the single person can remind everyone of the value of the present moment.

> In not knowing what tomorrow will bring, are not single persons well positioned to highlight the value of the present moment, precisely by showing that this present moment can be lived with and for God, in fidelity to his Word? As though the great emptiness experienced by single persons were calling for Christ's coming and caused them to pass from waiting to hope.[64]

[63] Ibid., 134.
[64] Ibid., 135.

Monastic life, priestly life, conjugal life, or the single life: acedia is a concern for all of us. Now every human being is created "in the image [of God], after [his] likeness" (Gen 1:26), and therefore feels in the depths of his soul an aspiration to the infinite, a desire that God alone can satisfy. Regrettably, very often he tries to satisfy that infinite desire with a series of goods or pleasures that in reality only exacerbate that desire and, ultimately, cause sadness and bitterness. Even in the case of someone who knows, by faith, that God alone can satisfy that desire, it sometimes happens that the infinite distance that separates the creature from the Creator plunges him into discouragement or even despair. For God remains on the heights. He is immensely great and far above us. That is man's first experience. Certainly, they tell us that man is made to encounter God, to be united with him, and even to share in his own life. But the distance seems infinite. The Creator of the universe, the One who governs everything, seems very far from us.

That is when something unexpected and unimaginable is revealed to us, which delivers us definitively from acedia: God bends down to the lowly. He sees us, he sees me. God's look upon the lowly is more than a simple look: it is also action. The fact that he sees me, that he looks at me, transforms me, just as it transforms the world around me. This, incidentally, is affirmed by the psalm: "He raises the poor from the dust" (Ps 113:7). By his look upon the lowly, God lifts me up; he benevolently takes me by the hand and helps me to get up from the depths and to move to higher ground. God humbles himself in order to raise me up.

This word from the psalm is a prophetic word. In the night of Bethlehem, it took on a completely new meaning. God's condescension was made real in a way that had been unprecedented and unimaginable before. God came as a baby, in the poverty of a stable. God really came down. He became an infant and placed himself in a state of vulnerability and total dependence, which is the condition of a newborn human being. The Creator who holds the whole world in his hands, on whom we all depend, became a little child in need of human love. God was born in a stable.

For God is endlessly resourceful. He saw that his greatness provoked resistance in man; he saw that man felt limited in his very being and threatened in his freedom. That is why he chose a new path. He became a child. He made himself dependent and weak, in need of our love. Henceforth—so this God who became a little child is telling us —you can no longer fear me; from now on you can only love me. That is why Saint John declares: "To all who received him, . . . he gave power to become children of God" (Jn 1:12).

God invites us to become his children. He calls us to set out on the way, to leave the self-containment of our desires and interests, in order to go out and meet him and adore him. God restores meaning to our life; he himself is "the way, and the truth, and the life" (Jn 14:6). Delivered from acedia, we are then invited to bring, in turn, the Good News of salvation to all our brethren!

CONCLUSION

The New Evangelization against Acedia

"Jesus, wearied as he was with his journey, sat down beside the well. It was about the sixth hour. There came a woman of Samaria to draw water" (Jn 4:6–7).

This woman who comes to the well at the "sixth hour", in other words, right at midday, an altogether unusual hour to go draw water, has a full-blown case of acedia. Why does she come at an hour like that? Because she does not want to be seen by others, because of the life that she is leading. The woman is torn. She is not living serenely. Humanly speaking, everything is a mess. She has had five husbands. She deeply desires love. But she realizes today that none of all she has gone in search of has fulfilled her. Although this "sixth hour" is the brightest hour, because the sun is at the zenith, the Samaritan woman is in a terrible dark night.

Now precisely at the moment when all hope seems to have disappeared, the Samaritan woman allows Jesus to meet her. He is "weary". This is a clear sign that he takes on our humanity. Jesus is hungry, also, since Saint John explains to us that there is some question about the food that the disciples went to buy. Jesus is actually in the same situation as the woman suffering from acedia, from the perspective of the frailty of his body. But his soul is not affected, since he says: "I have food to eat of which you do not know" (Jn 4:32).

By meeting this woman at the well, Jesus will turn her life completely upside-down. He reveals to her that she thirsts for a different kind of water from the one that she came to draw. Little by little he leads her to understand that he alone can satisfy that thirst in her. The Samaritan woman will go away rejoicing. She, who has come so as not to meet anyone, will from now on proclaim the man whom she met. Cured of her shame, she becomes a missionary and in her turn brings others to Jesus: "Come, see a man who told me all that I ever did!" (Jn 4:29). Precisely at the moment when she thinks that nothing can change any more, when it seems that she has come full circle in her life, her meeting with Christ becomes possible and everything is renewed for her.

As we conclude these pages, the staggering meeting of Jesus with the Samaritan woman presents to us a luminous path of conversion: from acedia is born the encounter with Christ; from that encounter, conversion is born; from conversion is born evangelization. But then, might not the new evangelization have something to tell us about our combat against acedia?

In October 2012, at the initiative of Pope Benedict XVI, the Synod of Bishops on the New Evangelization took place in Rome. It coincided with the opening of the Year of Faith, intended by the pope as a way of celebrating the fiftieth anniversary of the beginning of the Second Vatican Council. This expression, "new evangelization", coined by Pope John Paul II in Poland in 1979, corresponds to a deep desire of our Church to proclaim the Good News of salvation in Jesus Christ. As Benedict XVI explained, it is a question of making a second proclamation, although in reality it is always the same! More than ever, our countries of "old Christendom" need to recall that God loves them and wants to save them. Indeed:

> Recent decades have seen the advance of a spiritual "desertification". In the Council's time it was already possible from a few tragic pages of history to know what a life or a world without God looked like, but now we see it every day around us. This void has spread. But it is in starting from the experience of this desert, from this void, that we can again discover the joy of believing, its vital importance for us, men and women. In the desert we rediscover the value of what is essential for living; thus in today's world there are innumerable signs, often expressed implicitly or negatively, of the thirst for God, for the ultimate meaning of life. And in the desert people of faith are needed who, with their own lives, point out the way to the Promised Land and keep hope alive. Living faith opens the heart to the grace of God which frees us from pessimism. Today, more than ever, evangelizing means witnessing to the new life, transformed by God, and thus showing the path.[1]

These situations—spiritual desert, lack of joy and hope, general discouragement—are sometimes so tragic that they attack the very fiber of our Christian communities, subtly spreading the sickness of acedia, as Pope Paul VI already acknowledged.

[1] Benedict XVI, homily at Mass for the Opening of the Year of Faith (October 11, 2012).

Such obstacles [to evangelization] are also present today, and we shall limit ourselves to mentioning the lack of fervor. It is all the more serious because it comes from within. It is manifested in fatigue, disenchantment, compromise, lack of interest and above all lack of joy and hope.[2]

Therefore we urgently need to announce the Good News of salvation joyfully. To be a missionary is an integral part of our vocation as Christians. To proclaim Jesus, his mercy, salvation, and eternal life is the mission that our Lord gives to each of us on the day of his Ascension, at the moment when he returns to the Father: "Go therefore and make disciples of all nations" (Mt 28:19). Jesus truly is the way, the truth, and the life. In these difficult times, the Church invites us therefore to rediscover the foundations of our faith and of our Christian life. This is true for each one of us, and it is certainly true also for those who do not know God and whom we may meet. To care about evangelization is to care about salvation, ours and that of others; therefore it is a matter of eternal life! If whole sectors of our Christian civilization seem to be falling, it is because it is time to get to work and to facilitate the action of the Holy Spirit, the Spirit of truth and charity, so as to touch hearts and accomplish his work. Of course, the Lord is the one who brings about conversions, but he also willed to have need of us to announce him and to witness to him.

However, in this context, the new evangelization is proposed, not as a duty, an additional burden to carry, but as

[2] Paul VI, apostolic exhortation *Evangelii nuntiandi* (December 8, 1975), no. 80.

a remedy that can restore joy and life to realities that are imprisoned by our fears. This is why we must face the new evangelization boldly and enthusiastically.

> We exhort all those who have the task of evangelizing, by whatever title and at whatever level, always to nourish spiritual fervor. . . . Let us therefore preserve our fervor of spirit. Let us preserve the delightful and comforting joy of evangelizing, even when it is in tears that we must sow. May it mean for us—as it did for John the Baptist, for Peter and Paul, for the other apostles and for a multitude of splendid evangelizers all through the Church's history—an interior enthusiasm that nobody and nothing can quench. May it be the great joy of our consecrated lives. And may the world of our time, which is searching, sometimes with anguish, sometimes with hope, be enabled to receive the Good News not from evangelizers who are dejected, discouraged, impatient or anxious, but from ministers of the Gospel whose lives glow with fervor, who have first received the joy of Christ.[3]

We have had many occasions to say it in these pages: the chief remedy for acedia is found in the joy of the gift. A gift that precedes us, which is the gift of God himself who has come to be united with his creature, to share his weakness and poverty, so as to lead him to the ultimate goal of his existence: sharing in the very life of God. Now we can make this gift of God our own; we are called to enter into the same dynamism; we are called to give ourselves in turn. We are therefore invited to "go forth" from ourselves to bring the Good News to the whole world, a

[3] Ibid.

going-forth that is not so much geographical as existential and spiritual.

> Evangelizing presupposes that the Church has the freedom to go forth from herself. The Church is called to go out of herself in order to go to the peripheries, not only the geographical peripheries, but also the existential peripheries: to the dwelling places of the mystery of sin, suffering, injustices, ignorance and disdain for religion and thought, the dwelling places of all sorts of poverty.[4]

The Christian is a wayfarer—Saint Benedict even says that the monk must be a runner!—and, by that very fact, he cannot stop. We know very well: the equilibrium of walking lies in the uninterrupted concatenation of successive imbalances; each step is a divestment of self and an act of abandonment to the unknown. Each act of the Christian, whatever his state in life may be, must therefore also be a gift of self and an opening up to the Other, an abandonment to God who guides and directs our steps until we reach the house of the Father.

The "noonday devil" can be vanquished only by accepting the love of God and the sublimity of our vocation, which, in turn, gives rise to the joy of true Christian freedom. Therefore, to conclude, let us once again listen to the words of Pope Benedict XVI.

> Are we not perhaps all afraid in some way? If we let Christ enter fully into our lives, if we open ourselves totally to him, are we not afraid that He might take something away from us? Are we not perhaps afraid to give up something

[4] Jorge-Mario Cardinal Bergoglio, intervention during the general congregations preceding the 2013 conclave.

significant, something unique, something that makes life so beautiful? Do we not then risk ending up diminished and deprived of our freedom? . . . No! If we let Christ into our lives, we lose nothing, nothing, absolutely nothing of what makes life free, beautiful and great. No! Only in this friendship are the doors of life opened wide. Only in this friendship is the great potential of human existence truly revealed. Only in this friendship do we experience beauty and liberation.[5]

---

[5] Benedict XVI, homily at the Inaugural Mass of his Pontificate, April 24, 2005.

Select Bibliography

Bunge, Gabriel. *Despondency: The Spiritual Teaching of Evagrius of Pontus.* Yonkers: St. Vladimir's Seminary Press, 2012.

Forthomme, Bernard, *De l'acédie monastique à l'anxio-dépression: Histoire philosophique de la transformation d'un vice en pathologie.* Paris: Sanofi-Synthélabo, 2000.

Nabert, Nathalie, ed. *Tristesse, acédie et médecine de âmes.* Spiritualité cartusienne. Paris: Beauchesne, 2005.

Nault, Jean-Charles. *La saveur de Dieu: L'acédie dans le dynamisme de l'agir.* Cogitatio Fidei 248. Paris: Cerf, 2006.

Ratzinger, Joseph. *To Look on Christ: Exercises in Faith, Hope and Love.* Translated by Robert Nowell. New York: Crossroad, 1991.